50 Food Truck Recipes for Home

By: Kelly Johnson

Table of Contents

- Gourmet Grilled Cheese
- Korean BBQ Tacos
- Pulled Pork Sandwiches
- Buffalo Chicken Wraps
- Mediterranean Falafel Pitas
- Fish Tacos with Mango Salsa
- Philly Cheesesteak Sandwiches
- Cajun Shrimp Po'Boys
- BBQ Pulled Chicken Sliders
- Vegetarian Quesadillas
- Hawaiian Teriyaki Chicken Bowls
- Cuban Sandwiches
- Greek Gyro Wraps
- Loaded Nachos
- Thai Green Curry Noodle Bowl
- Mexican Street Corn (Elote)
- BBQ Brisket Tacos
- Spicy Chicken Wings
- Italian Meatball Subs
- Vietnamese Banh Mi Sandwiches
- Breakfast Burritos
- Cajun Crawfish Boil
- Beef Bulgogi Tacos
- Indian Butter Chicken Wraps
- Classic Cheeseburgers
- Buffalo Cauliflower Bites
- Cuban Mojo Pork Tacos
- Southern Fried Chicken Sandwiches
- Japanese Ramen Noodle Soup
- Philly Cheesesteak Egg Rolls
- Pulled Pork Mac and Cheese
- Vegetarian Falafel Wraps
- Hawaiian Poke Bowls
- Korean Kimchi Fries
- Chicken Shawarma Pitas

- Thai Basil Chicken Rice Bowl
- Mexican Churros with Chocolate Sauce
- Cuban Tostones with Garlic Sauce
- Greek Souvlaki Skewers
- Korean Bibimbap Bowls
- BBQ Rib Sliders
- Vegetarian Spring Rolls with Peanut Sauce
- Cajun Gumbo
- Beef Barbacoa Tacos
- Vietnamese Pho Soup
- Loaded Tater Tots
- Jerk Chicken Wraps
- Caprese Panini
- Hawaiian Spam Musubi
- Thai Mango Sticky Rice

Gourmet Grilled Cheese

Ingredients:

- 4 slices of your favorite bread (sourdough, whole wheat, etc.)
- 2 tablespoons unsalted butter, softened
- 1 cup shredded cheese (use a combination of your favorite cheeses such as cheddar, mozzarella, Swiss, Gruyere, etc.)
- 2 slices of cooked bacon (optional)
- 1/2 avocado, sliced
- 1/4 cup caramelized onions (optional)
- 1 tablespoon honey (optional)
- Pinch of salt and pepper

Instructions:

1. Preheat Pan: Heat a skillet or griddle over medium heat.
2. Butter Bread: Spread a thin layer of softened butter on one side of each slice of bread.
3. Assemble Sandwich: Place two slices of bread, buttered side down, on a clean surface. Layer each slice with shredded cheese, cooked bacon (if using), avocado slices, caramelized onions (if using), and a drizzle of honey (if using). Season with a pinch of salt and pepper.
4. Close Sandwich: Place the remaining slices of bread on top, buttered side facing up.
5. Grill Sandwich: Carefully transfer the assembled sandwiches to the preheated skillet or griddle. Cook for 3-4 minutes on each side, or until the bread is golden brown and crispy, and the cheese is melted.
6. Serve: Remove the grilled cheese sandwiches from the skillet or griddle and let them cool for a minute before slicing them in half. Serve immediately and enjoy!

This gourmet grilled cheese is a delicious twist on the classic comfort food. The combination of gooey melted cheese, creamy avocado, savory bacon, and sweet caramelized onions creates a flavor explosion that will satisfy your taste buds. Serve it with a side of tomato soup for the ultimate comfort meal.

Korean BBQ Tacos

Ingredients:

For the Korean BBQ Beef:

- 1 lb beef sirloin or flank steak, thinly sliced
- 1/4 cup soy sauce
- 2 tablespoons brown sugar
- 2 cloves garlic, minced
- 1 tablespoon sesame oil
- 1 tablespoon rice vinegar
- 1 teaspoon fresh ginger, grated
- 2 green onions, thinly sliced
- 1 tablespoon vegetable oil, for cooking

For the Tacos:

- 8 small flour or corn tortillas
- 1 cup shredded cabbage
- 1/2 cup matchstick carrots
- 1/4 cup chopped fresh cilantro
- 1 tablespoon sesame seeds (optional)
- Sriracha or Korean chili paste (gochujang), for serving (optional)

Instructions:

1. Marinate the Beef: In a bowl, combine soy sauce, brown sugar, minced garlic, sesame oil, rice vinegar, grated ginger, and sliced green onions. Add the thinly sliced beef to the marinade, cover, and refrigerate for at least 1 hour, or overnight for best flavor.
2. Cook the Beef: Heat vegetable oil in a large skillet or grill pan over medium-high heat. Remove the beef from the marinade, shaking off any excess, and cook in batches for 2-3 minutes per side, or until browned and cooked through. Transfer cooked beef to a plate and set aside.
3. Warm the Tortillas: Heat the tortillas in a dry skillet or wrap them in foil and warm in the oven until soft and pliable.
4. Assemble the Tacos: Fill each tortilla with a portion of the cooked Korean BBQ beef. Top with shredded cabbage, matchstick carrots, chopped cilantro, and a sprinkle of sesame seeds.

5. Serve: Serve the Korean BBQ tacos immediately, with Sriracha or Korean chili paste (gochujang) on the side for extra heat, if desired.

These Korean BBQ tacos are a delicious fusion of flavors, combining tender marinated beef with crunchy vegetables and fresh herbs. They make a perfect meal for a casual dinner or a fun taco night with friends and family. Enjoy the bold and savory taste of Korean cuisine in a convenient and handheld taco form!

Pulled Pork Sandwiches

Ingredients:

For the Pulled Pork:

- 3-4 lbs pork shoulder (also known as pork butt)
- 2 tablespoons brown sugar
- 1 tablespoon paprika
- 1 tablespoon garlic powder
- 1 tablespoon onion powder
- 1 teaspoon ground cumin
- 1 teaspoon chili powder
- 1 teaspoon salt
- 1/2 teaspoon black pepper
- 1 cup chicken or vegetable broth
- 1/2 cup apple cider vinegar
- 1/4 cup barbecue sauce (plus extra for serving)
- Sandwich buns or rolls

For the Coleslaw (optional topping):

- 2 cups shredded cabbage or coleslaw mix
- 1/4 cup mayonnaise
- 1 tablespoon apple cider vinegar
- 1 teaspoon sugar
- Salt and pepper to taste

Instructions:

1. Prepare the Pork: In a small bowl, mix together the brown sugar, paprika, garlic powder, onion powder, cumin, chili powder, salt, and black pepper to create a dry rub. Rub the mixture all over the pork shoulder, covering it evenly. Let the pork sit at room temperature for 30 minutes to allow the flavors to penetrate.
2. Cook the Pork: Preheat your oven to 325°F (163°C). Place the pork shoulder in a roasting pan or Dutch oven. Pour the chicken or vegetable broth and apple cider vinegar around the pork. Cover the pan tightly with aluminum foil or a lid. Roast the pork in the preheated oven for 3-4 hours, or until the meat is tender and easily pulls apart with a fork.
3. Shred the Pork: Once the pork is cooked, remove it from the oven and let it rest for a few minutes. Use two forks to shred the meat, discarding any excess fat.

4. Finish the Pulled Pork: In a large skillet or saucepan, combine the shredded pork with barbecue sauce. Cook over medium heat for 5-10 minutes, stirring occasionally, until the pork is heated through and the sauce is evenly distributed.
5. Prepare the Coleslaw (optional): In a mixing bowl, combine the shredded cabbage or coleslaw mix with mayonnaise, apple cider vinegar, sugar, salt, and pepper. Toss until well coated.
6. Assemble the Sandwiches: To assemble the pulled pork sandwiches, place a generous portion of the pulled pork on the bottom half of each sandwich bun or roll. Top with a spoonful of coleslaw, if desired. Place the top half of the bun on top of the pork.
7. Serve: Serve the pulled pork sandwiches immediately, with extra barbecue sauce on the side for dipping, if desired.

These pulled pork sandwiches are a classic comfort food favorite, perfect for casual gatherings, game day parties, or weeknight dinners. The tender and flavorful pork, paired with the tangy coleslaw and soft sandwich buns, is sure to be a hit with everyone at the table. Enjoy the deliciousness of homemade pulled pork sandwiches any time you crave a hearty and satisfying meal!

Buffalo Chicken Wraps

Ingredients:

For the Buffalo Chicken:

- 2 boneless, skinless chicken breasts
- Salt and pepper, to taste
- 1/2 cup buffalo sauce
- 2 tablespoons unsalted butter, melted

For the Wraps:

- 4 large flour tortillas or wraps
- 1 cup shredded lettuce
- 1 cup diced tomatoes
- 1/2 cup crumbled blue cheese or shredded mozzarella cheese
- Ranch or blue cheese dressing, for drizzling (optional)

Instructions:

1. Cook the Chicken: Season the chicken breasts with salt and pepper on both sides. Heat a grill pan or skillet over medium-high heat and cook the chicken for 6-8 minutes per side, or until cooked through and no longer pink in the center. Alternatively, you can bake the chicken in a preheated oven at 375°F (190°C) for 20-25 minutes, or until cooked through. Once cooked, let the chicken rest for a few minutes, then shred it using two forks.
2. Prepare the Buffalo Sauce: In a small bowl, mix together the buffalo sauce and melted butter. Pour the sauce over the shredded chicken and toss until evenly coated.
3. Assemble the Wraps: Lay out the flour tortillas or wraps on a clean surface. Divide the shredded lettuce, diced tomatoes, and crumbled blue cheese evenly among the tortillas, placing the ingredients in the center of each wrap. Spoon the buffalo chicken mixture on top of the vegetables and cheese.
4. Drizzle with Dressing (Optional): If desired, drizzle ranch or blue cheese dressing over the buffalo chicken mixture.
5. Wrap the Wraps: Fold the sides of each tortilla in towards the center, then roll up tightly from the bottom to form a wrap.
6. Serve: Serve the buffalo chicken wraps immediately, or wrap them tightly in foil for easy transport or storage.

These buffalo chicken wraps are perfect for a quick and flavorful lunch or dinner. The spicy buffalo chicken, crisp lettuce, juicy tomatoes, and tangy blue cheese come together to create a delicious and satisfying meal that's sure to please your taste buds. Enjoy the bold flavors of buffalo chicken in a convenient handheld wrap!

Mediterranean Falafel Pitas

Ingredients:

For the Falafel:

- 1 can (15 oz) chickpeas, drained and rinsed
- 1/2 cup chopped fresh parsley
- 1/4 cup chopped fresh cilantro
- 1/4 cup chopped onion
- 2 cloves garlic, minced
- 1 teaspoon ground cumin
- 1 teaspoon ground coriander
- 1/2 teaspoon salt
- 1/4 teaspoon black pepper
- 2 tablespoons all-purpose flour or chickpea flour
- Vegetable oil, for frying

For the Tzatziki Sauce:

- 1 cup Greek yogurt
- 1/2 cucumber, grated and squeezed to remove excess moisture
- 1 clove garlic, minced
- 1 tablespoon chopped fresh dill (or 1 teaspoon dried dill)
- 1 tablespoon lemon juice
- Salt and pepper, to taste

For Assembling:

- 4 pita bread rounds, warmed
- Thinly sliced red onion
- Sliced tomatoes
- Chopped lettuce or mixed greens
- Crumbled feta cheese (optional)
- Kalamata olives, pitted and chopped (optional)

Instructions:

1. Prepare the Falafel Mixture: In a food processor, combine the chickpeas, parsley, cilantro, onion, garlic, cumin, coriander, salt, and pepper. Pulse until the mixture is finely chopped but not completely smooth. Transfer the mixture to a bowl and stir

in the flour until well combined. If the mixture seems too wet, add more flour as needed.
2. Shape the Falafel: Using your hands, shape the falafel mixture into small patties, about 1 1/2 inches in diameter and 1/2 inch thick.
3. Fry the Falafel: Heat vegetable oil in a large skillet over medium heat. Carefully add the falafel patties to the skillet in batches, making sure not to overcrowd the pan. Cook for 3-4 minutes per side, or until golden brown and crispy. Transfer the cooked falafel to a paper towel-lined plate to drain any excess oil.
4. Prepare the Tzatziki Sauce: In a small bowl, combine the Greek yogurt, grated cucumber, minced garlic, chopped dill, lemon juice, salt, and pepper. Stir until well combined. Adjust seasoning to taste.
5. Assemble the Pitas: Warm the pita bread rounds in the oven or microwave. Cut each pita in half to form pockets. Stuff each pita pocket with falafel patties, sliced red onion, sliced tomatoes, chopped lettuce or mixed greens, crumbled feta cheese (if using), and chopped Kalamata olives (if using). Drizzle with tzatziki sauce.
6. Serve: Serve the Mediterranean falafel pitas immediately, while the falafel is still warm and crispy.

These Mediterranean falafel pitas are packed with flavor and texture, making them a satisfying and delicious meal option. Enjoy the combination of crispy falafel, tangy tzatziki sauce, and fresh veggies in each bite!

Fish Tacos with Mango Salsa

Ingredients:

For the Fish:

- 1 lb white fish fillets (such as cod, tilapia, or mahi-mahi)
- 2 tablespoons olive oil
- 1 tablespoon lime juice
- 1 teaspoon chili powder
- 1/2 teaspoon ground cumin
- Salt and pepper, to taste

For the Mango Salsa:

- 1 ripe mango, peeled, pitted, and diced
- 1/2 red onion, finely chopped
- 1/2 red bell pepper, diced
- 1 jalapeño pepper, seeded and minced
- 1/4 cup chopped fresh cilantro
- 1 tablespoon lime juice
- Salt and pepper, to taste

For Assembling:

- 8 small corn tortillas, warmed
- Shredded cabbage or coleslaw mix
- Avocado slices
- Lime wedges
- Additional cilantro, for garnish (optional)

Instructions:

1. Prepare the Fish: In a small bowl, mix together the olive oil, lime juice, chili powder, cumin, salt, and pepper. Place the fish fillets in a shallow dish and pour the marinade over them, turning to coat evenly. Let the fish marinate for 15-30 minutes.
2. Cook the Fish: Heat a grill pan or skillet over medium-high heat. Remove the fish from the marinade and cook for 3-4 minutes per side, or until cooked through and flaky. Remove from heat and let cool slightly. Use a fork to flake the fish into bite-sized pieces.

3. Prepare the Mango Salsa: In a medium bowl, combine the diced mango, chopped red onion, diced red bell pepper, minced jalapeño pepper, chopped cilantro, lime juice, salt, and pepper. Stir until well combined. Adjust seasoning to taste.
4. Assemble the Tacos: Fill each warmed corn tortilla with a portion of the shredded cabbage or coleslaw mix, followed by the flaked fish, and a spoonful of mango salsa. Top with avocado slices and additional cilantro, if desired. Serve with lime wedges on the side.
5. Serve: Serve the fish tacos with mango salsa immediately, allowing everyone to customize their tacos with their favorite toppings.

These fish tacos with mango salsa are bursting with fresh flavors and vibrant colors, making them a perfect choice for a light and flavorful meal. Enjoy the combination of tender fish, sweet and tangy mango salsa, and crunchy cabbage in each bite!

Philly Cheesesteak Sandwiches

Ingredients:

- 1 lb ribeye steak, thinly sliced
- 2 tablespoons vegetable oil
- 1 onion, thinly sliced
- 1 green bell pepper, thinly sliced
- 4 hoagie rolls or sub rolls
- 8 slices provolone cheese
- Salt and pepper, to taste

Instructions:

1. Cook the Steak: Heat a large skillet over medium-high heat. Add 1 tablespoon of vegetable oil to the skillet. Season the thinly sliced ribeye steak with salt and pepper. Add the steak slices to the skillet and cook for 2-3 minutes per side, or until browned and cooked to your desired level of doneness. Remove the cooked steak from the skillet and set aside.
2. Cook the Vegetables: In the same skillet, add the remaining tablespoon of vegetable oil. Add the thinly sliced onion and green bell pepper to the skillet. Cook, stirring occasionally, for 5-6 minutes, or until the vegetables are tender and slightly caramelized.
3. Assemble the Sandwiches: Preheat the oven to 350°F (175°C). Slice the hoagie rolls or sub rolls in half lengthwise, without cutting all the way through. Place two slices of provolone cheese on the bottom half of each roll. Top the cheese with a portion of the cooked steak, followed by a portion of the cooked onions and green peppers. Place two more slices of provolone cheese on top of the vegetables. Close the sandwiches with the top halves of the rolls.
4. Bake the Sandwiches: Place the assembled sandwiches on a baking sheet and bake in the preheated oven for 5-7 minutes, or until the cheese is melted and bubbly.
5. Serve: Remove the Philly cheesesteak sandwiches from the oven and let them cool slightly. Serve warm and enjoy!

These Philly cheesesteak sandwiches are loaded with tender ribeye steak, sautéed onions, green peppers, and melted provolone cheese, all nestled inside a soft and crusty hoagie roll. They make for a delicious and satisfying meal that's perfect for lunch or dinner!

Cajun Shrimp Po'Boys

Ingredients:

For the Cajun Shrimp:

- 1 lb large shrimp, peeled and deveined
- 2 tablespoons Cajun seasoning
- 2 tablespoons olive oil

For the Remoulade Sauce:

- 1/2 cup mayonnaise
- 2 tablespoons ketchup
- 1 tablespoon Dijon mustard
- 1 tablespoon lemon juice
- 1 clove garlic, minced
- 1 teaspoon Worcestershire sauce
- 1/2 teaspoon hot sauce (optional)
- Salt and pepper, to taste

For Assembling:

- 4 hoagie rolls or French bread, sliced
- Shredded lettuce
- Sliced tomatoes
- Sliced pickles
- Sliced red onion (optional)
- Lemon wedges, for serving

Instructions:

1. Prepare the Cajun Shrimp: In a large bowl, toss the peeled and deveined shrimp with Cajun seasoning until evenly coated. Heat olive oil in a large skillet over medium-high heat. Add the seasoned shrimp to the skillet and cook for 2-3 minutes per side, or until pink and cooked through. Remove from heat and set aside.
2. Make the Remoulade Sauce: In a small bowl, whisk together mayonnaise, ketchup, Dijon mustard, lemon juice, minced garlic, Worcestershire sauce, hot sauce (if using), salt, and pepper until smooth and well combined. Adjust seasoning to taste.

3. Assemble the Po'Boys: Spread a generous amount of remoulade sauce on each sliced hoagie roll or French bread. Layer shredded lettuce, sliced tomatoes, sliced pickles, and cooked Cajun shrimp on top of the sauce. Add sliced red onion, if desired. Close the sandwiches with the top halves of the rolls.
4. Serve: Serve the Cajun shrimp po'boys immediately, with lemon wedges on the side for squeezing over the sandwiches.

These Cajun shrimp po'boys are packed with flavor and texture, making them a delicious and satisfying meal option. Enjoy the spicy Cajun shrimp, tangy remoulade sauce, and crisp veggies nestled inside a soft and crusty hoagie roll!

BBQ Pulled Chicken Sliders

Ingredients:

For the Pulled Chicken:

- 2 lbs boneless, skinless chicken breasts
- 1 cup barbecue sauce
- 1/4 cup chicken broth or water
- 2 tablespoons brown sugar
- 1 tablespoon apple cider vinegar
- 1 teaspoon garlic powder
- 1 teaspoon onion powder
- 1/2 teaspoon smoked paprika
- Salt and pepper, to taste

For Assembling:

- Slider buns or dinner rolls
- Coleslaw (optional)
- Pickles (optional)
- Red onion slices (optional)

Instructions:

1. Cook the Chicken: Place the chicken breasts in the slow cooker. In a bowl, mix together the barbecue sauce, chicken broth or water, brown sugar, apple cider vinegar, garlic powder, onion powder, smoked paprika, salt, and pepper. Pour the sauce mixture over the chicken breasts, making sure they are well coated. Cover and cook on low for 6-8 hours or on high for 3-4 hours, until the chicken is tender and easily shreds with a fork.
2. Shred the Chicken: Once the chicken is cooked, use two forks to shred it directly in the slow cooker. Mix the shredded chicken with the sauce to coat evenly. Keep warm in the slow cooker until ready to serve.
3. Assemble the Sliders: Split the slider buns or dinner rolls and place a spoonful of pulled chicken on the bottom half of each bun. Add coleslaw, pickles, and red onion slices on top of the chicken, if desired. Place the top half of the bun over the filling to complete the sliders.
4. Serve: Arrange the BBQ pulled chicken sliders on a serving platter and serve immediately.

These BBQ pulled chicken sliders are perfect for parties, gatherings, or even weeknight dinners. The tender and flavorful pulled chicken, combined with the sweet and tangy barbecue sauce, is sure to be a hit with everyone! Customize with your favorite toppings and enjoy the deliciousness of these sliders.

Vegetarian Quesadillas

Ingredients:

- 4 large flour tortillas
- 1 cup black beans, drained and rinsed
- 1 cup corn kernels (fresh, canned, or frozen)
- 1 bell pepper, diced
- 1 small red onion, diced
- 1 jalapeño pepper, seeded and diced (optional)
- 1 cup shredded cheese (cheddar, Monterey Jack, or Mexican blend)
- 1 teaspoon ground cumin
- 1 teaspoon chili powder
- Salt and pepper, to taste
- Olive oil or cooking spray, for cooking
- Sour cream, salsa, guacamole, or your favorite dipping sauce, for serving

Instructions:

1. Prepare the Filling: In a large skillet, heat a drizzle of olive oil over medium heat. Add the diced bell pepper, red onion, and jalapeño pepper (if using). Cook for 5-6 minutes, or until the vegetables are softened and slightly caramelized. Add the black beans, corn kernels, ground cumin, chili powder, salt, and pepper to the skillet. Stir to combine and cook for an additional 2-3 minutes. Remove from heat and set aside.
2. Assemble the Quesadillas: Lay out the flour tortillas on a clean surface. Divide the shredded cheese evenly among the tortillas, spreading it out over one half of each tortilla. Spoon the vegetable and bean mixture over the cheese, then fold the other half of the tortilla over the filling to create a half-moon shape.
3. Cook the Quesadillas: Heat a large skillet or griddle over medium heat. Lightly grease the skillet with olive oil or cooking spray. Carefully transfer the assembled quesadillas to the skillet and cook for 2-3 minutes per side, or until the tortillas are golden brown and crispy, and the cheese is melted.
4. Serve: Remove the cooked quesadillas from the skillet and let them cool for a minute before slicing into wedges. Serve warm with sour cream, salsa, guacamole, or your favorite dipping sauce on the side.

These vegetarian quesadillas are loaded with flavorful black beans, sweet corn, sautéed peppers, onions, and melted cheese, all wrapped in a crispy tortilla shell. They make a delicious and satisfying meal or snack that's perfect for lunch, dinner, or anytime you're craving a cheesy, melty treat!

Hawaiian Teriyaki Chicken Bowls

Ingredients:

For the Teriyaki Chicken:

- 1 lb boneless, skinless chicken breasts, cut into bite-sized pieces
- 1/2 cup teriyaki sauce
- 2 tablespoons soy sauce
- 2 cloves garlic, minced
- 1 tablespoon brown sugar
- 1 tablespoon sesame oil
- 1 tablespoon cornstarch
- 2 tablespoons water
- Pineapple chunks (fresh or canned), for serving

For the Pineapple Salsa:

- 1 cup diced fresh pineapple
- 1/2 red bell pepper, diced
- 1/4 red onion, finely chopped
- 1 tablespoon chopped cilantro
- 1 tablespoon lime juice
- Salt and pepper, to taste

For Assembling:

- Cooked white or brown rice
- Sliced green onions, for garnish
- Sesame seeds, for garnish

Instructions:

1. Marinate the Chicken: In a bowl, combine teriyaki sauce, soy sauce, minced garlic, brown sugar, and sesame oil. Add the bite-sized chicken pieces to the marinade and toss to coat. Cover and refrigerate for at least 30 minutes, or up to 2 hours.
2. Prepare the Pineapple Salsa: In another bowl, combine diced pineapple, diced red bell pepper, finely chopped red onion, chopped cilantro, lime juice, salt, and pepper. Stir to combine. Cover and refrigerate until ready to use.

3. Cook the Chicken: Heat a large skillet or wok over medium-high heat. Remove the marinated chicken from the refrigerator and drain off any excess marinade. Add the chicken pieces to the hot skillet and cook for 6-8 minutes, stirring occasionally, or until the chicken is cooked through and browned on all sides.
4. Make the Teriyaki Sauce: In a small bowl, mix together cornstarch and water to create a slurry. Add the slurry to the skillet with the cooked chicken, along with any remaining marinade. Cook, stirring constantly, for 1-2 minutes, or until the sauce has thickened and coats the chicken evenly.
5. Assemble the Bowls: Divide cooked rice among serving bowls. Top each bowl with teriyaki chicken, pineapple salsa, and pineapple chunks. Garnish with sliced green onions and sesame seeds.
6. Serve: Serve the Hawaiian teriyaki chicken bowls immediately, and enjoy!

These Hawaiian teriyaki chicken bowls are a delicious combination of sweet and savory flavors, with tender teriyaki chicken, juicy pineapple salsa, and fluffy rice. They're easy to make and perfect for a quick and satisfying meal!

Cuban Sandwiches

Ingredients:

- 1 loaf Cuban bread or French bread, sliced horizontally
- 1/2 lb roasted pork loin or ham, thinly sliced
- 1/2 lb Swiss cheese, thinly sliced
- 1/2 lb cooked ham, thinly sliced
- Dill pickles, sliced lengthwise
- Yellow mustard
- Butter, softened

Instructions:

1. Preheat the Panini Press: If you have a panini press, preheat it to medium-high heat. If you don't have a panini press, you can use a skillet or griddle on the stovetop.
2. Assemble the Sandwiches: Spread a thin layer of mustard on one half of the bread slices. Layer the roasted pork loin or ham, Swiss cheese, cooked ham, and dill pickles on top of the mustard. Close the sandwiches with the remaining bread slices.
3. Butter the Bread: Spread a thin layer of softened butter on the outside of each sandwich.
4. Cook the Sandwiches: Place the sandwiches on the preheated panini press or skillet. If using a panini press, close the lid and cook for 5-7 minutes, or until the bread is golden brown and crispy, and the cheese is melted. If using a skillet, place a heavy pan or skillet on top of the sandwiches to press them down. Cook for 3-4 minutes on each side, or until the bread is golden brown and crispy, and the cheese is melted. Flip the sandwiches halfway through cooking.
5. Serve: Remove the cooked Cuban sandwiches from the panini press or skillet. Let them cool for a minute, then slice them diagonally into halves or quarters. Serve immediately, and enjoy!

These Cuban sandwiches are a classic combination of flavors, with tender roasted pork or ham, Swiss cheese, tangy pickles, and mustard, all pressed between slices of crusty bread. They're perfect for a quick and satisfying lunch or dinner!

Greek Gyro Wraps

Ingredients:

For the Gyro Meat:

- 1 lb ground lamb or beef
- 1 small onion, grated
- 2 cloves garlic, minced
- 1 teaspoon dried oregano
- 1 teaspoon dried thyme
- 1 teaspoon ground cumin
- 1/2 teaspoon ground coriander
- Salt and pepper, to taste

For the Tzatziki Sauce:

- 1 cup Greek yogurt
- 1/2 cucumber, grated and squeezed to remove excess moisture
- 1 clove garlic, minced
- 1 tablespoon chopped fresh dill (or 1 teaspoon dried dill)
- 1 tablespoon lemon juice
- Salt and pepper, to taste

For Assembling:

- 4 large pita bread rounds or flatbreads
- Thinly sliced tomatoes
- Thinly sliced red onion
- Shredded lettuce or chopped romaine
- Crumbled feta cheese (optional)
- Kalamata olives, pitted and chopped (optional)

Instructions:

1. Prepare the Gyro Meat: In a large bowl, combine the ground lamb or beef with grated onion, minced garlic, dried oregano, dried thyme, ground cumin, ground coriander, salt, and pepper. Mix until well combined. Shape the mixture into small, thin patties.

2. Cook the Gyro Meat: Heat a grill pan or skillet over medium-high heat. Cook the gyro patties for 3-4 minutes per side, or until cooked through and browned. Remove from heat and set aside.
3. Prepare the Tzatziki Sauce: In a small bowl, combine Greek yogurt, grated cucumber, minced garlic, chopped dill, lemon juice, salt, and pepper. Stir until well combined. Adjust seasoning to taste.
4. Assemble the Gyro Wraps: Warm the pita bread rounds or flatbreads. Spread a generous amount of tzatziki sauce on each bread. Top with cooked gyro meat, thinly sliced tomatoes, thinly sliced red onion, shredded lettuce or chopped romaine, crumbled feta cheese (if using), and chopped Kalamata olives (if using).
5. Wrap the Gyros: Fold the sides of each pita bread over the filling, then roll up tightly from the bottom to form a wrap.
6. Serve: Serve the Greek gyro wraps immediately, while warm. Enjoy!

These Greek gyro wraps are packed with flavorful gyro meat, tangy tzatziki sauce, and fresh veggies, all wrapped up in warm pita bread. They make for a delicious and satisfying meal that's perfect for lunch or dinner!

Loaded Nachos

Ingredients:

- 1 bag (about 10-12 oz) tortilla chips
- 1 lb ground beef or turkey
- 1 packet taco seasoning
- 1 cup shredded cheddar cheese
- 1 cup shredded Monterey Jack cheese
- 1 cup black beans, drained and rinsed
- 1 cup corn kernels (fresh, canned, or frozen)
- 1/2 cup diced tomatoes
- 1/4 cup sliced black olives
- 1/4 cup chopped green onions
- 1/4 cup chopped fresh cilantro
- 1 jalapeño pepper, sliced (optional)
- Sour cream, guacamole, salsa, and/or hot sauce, for serving

Instructions:

1. Preheat the Oven: Preheat your oven to 375°F (190°C).
2. Cook the Ground Meat: In a skillet over medium heat, cook the ground beef or turkey until browned and cooked through. Drain any excess grease. Add the taco seasoning and cook according to the packet instructions. Remove from heat and set aside.
3. Assemble the Nachos: Spread the tortilla chips in a single layer on a large baking sheet or oven-safe platter. Sprinkle half of the shredded cheddar cheese and half of the shredded Monterey Jack cheese evenly over the chips. Top with the cooked ground meat, black beans, corn kernels, diced tomatoes, sliced black olives, and sliced jalapeño peppers (if using). Sprinkle the remaining shredded cheese on top.
4. Bake the Nachos: Place the loaded nachos in the preheated oven and bake for 10-12 minutes, or until the cheese is melted and bubbly.
5. Garnish and Serve: Remove the nachos from the oven and sprinkle chopped green onions and fresh cilantro over the top. Serve the loaded nachos hot with sour cream, guacamole, salsa, and/or hot sauce on the side for dipping.
6. Enjoy: Serve the loaded nachos immediately, and enjoy!

These loaded nachos are perfect for game day, movie night, or anytime you're craving a delicious and satisfying snack. Customize them with your favorite toppings and enjoy the cheesy, crunchy goodness!

Thai Green Curry Noodle Bowl

Ingredients:

For the Green Curry Paste:

- 2 green chilies, chopped
- 2 shallots, chopped
- 3 cloves garlic, minced
- 1 stalk lemongrass, chopped
- 1-inch piece ginger, chopped
- 1 teaspoon ground coriander
- 1/2 teaspoon ground cumin
- 1/2 teaspoon ground turmeric
- 1/2 teaspoon shrimp paste (optional)
- Zest of 1 lime
- 2 tablespoons chopped fresh cilantro stems

For the Noodle Bowl:

- 8 oz rice noodles
- 1 tablespoon vegetable oil
- 1 can (13.5 oz) coconut milk
- 2 cups vegetable broth
- 1 tablespoon soy sauce
- 1 tablespoon brown sugar
- 1 cup mixed vegetables (such as bell peppers, broccoli, carrots, and snow peas)
- 1 cup tofu or cooked chicken, sliced
- Fresh cilantro leaves, for garnish
- Lime wedges, for serving

Instructions:

1. Make the Green Curry Paste: In a blender or food processor, combine the chopped green chilies, shallots, garlic, lemongrass, ginger, ground coriander, ground cumin, ground turmeric, shrimp paste (if using), lime zest, and chopped cilantro stems. Blend until a smooth paste forms. Set aside.
2. Cook the Rice Noodles: Cook the rice noodles according to the package instructions. Drain and set aside.

3. Prepare the Curry Base: In a large pot or wok, heat the vegetable oil over medium heat. Add 2-3 tablespoons of the green curry paste (reserve the rest for future use) and cook for 1-2 minutes, stirring constantly, until fragrant.
4. Add Coconut Milk and Broth: Pour in the coconut milk and vegetable broth. Stir to combine and bring the mixture to a simmer.
5. Season and Add Vegetables: Stir in the soy sauce and brown sugar. Add the mixed vegetables and sliced tofu or cooked chicken. Cook for 5-7 minutes, or until the vegetables are tender and the protein is heated through.
6. Assemble the Noodle Bowl: Divide the cooked rice noodles among serving bowls. Ladle the hot curry broth and vegetables over the noodles.
7. Garnish and Serve: Garnish the Thai green curry noodle bowls with fresh cilantro leaves and serve with lime wedges on the side.
8. Enjoy: Serve the Thai green curry noodle bowls hot, and enjoy!

These Thai green curry noodle bowls are aromatic, flavorful, and packed with delicious ingredients. They make for a satisfying and comforting meal that's perfect for any day of the week!

Mexican Street Corn (Elote)

Ingredients:

- 4 ears of corn, husks removed
- 1/4 cup mayonnaise
- 1/4 cup sour cream or Mexican crema
- 1/2 cup crumbled cotija cheese or feta cheese
- 1 teaspoon chili powder
- 1/4 cup chopped fresh cilantro (optional)
- Lime wedges, for serving

Instructions:

1. Grill the Corn: Preheat your grill to medium-high heat. Place the ears of corn directly on the grill grates and cook, turning occasionally, for 8-10 minutes, or until the corn is tender and lightly charred on all sides.
2. Prepare the Toppings: In a small bowl, mix together the mayonnaise and sour cream or Mexican crema until well combined.
3. Coat the Corn: Remove the grilled corn from the grill and brush each ear with the mayonnaise and sour cream mixture, using a pastry brush or spoon to coat evenly.
4. Add Cheese and Seasoning: Sprinkle the crumbled cotija cheese or feta cheese over the mayonnaise mixture, rolling each ear of corn in the cheese to coat evenly. Sprinkle chili powder over the cheese, to taste.
5. Garnish and Serve: Garnish the Mexican street corn with chopped fresh cilantro, if desired. Serve hot with lime wedges on the side for squeezing over the corn.
6. Enjoy: Serve the Mexican street corn (elote) immediately, and enjoy!

This Mexican street corn recipe is a classic street food favorite, featuring grilled corn coated with creamy mayonnaise, tangy sour cream or crema, salty cotija cheese or feta cheese, and zesty chili powder. It's a delicious and flavorful dish that's perfect for summer cookouts, picnics, or anytime you're craving a taste of Mexico!

BBQ Brisket Tacos

Ingredients:

For the Brisket:

- 2 lbs beef brisket
- Salt and pepper, to taste
- 1 tablespoon vegetable oil
- 1 cup barbecue sauce

For the Tacos:

- 8-10 small corn or flour tortillas
- 1 cup shredded lettuce or cabbage
- 1 cup diced tomatoes
- 1/2 cup diced red onion
- 1/2 cup chopped fresh cilantro
- Lime wedges, for serving
- Additional barbecue sauce, for drizzling (optional)

Instructions:

1. Prepare the Brisket: Preheat your oven to 300°F (150°C). Season the beef brisket generously with salt and pepper. Heat vegetable oil in a large skillet or Dutch oven over medium-high heat. Sear the brisket on all sides until browned, about 3-4 minutes per side. Transfer the brisket to a roasting pan or baking dish. Pour barbecue sauce over the brisket, covering it evenly. Cover the pan tightly with foil and roast in the preheated oven for 3-4 hours, or until the brisket is tender and easily shreds with a fork.
2. Shred the Brisket: Remove the brisket from the oven and let it rest for a few minutes. Use two forks to shred the brisket into bite-sized pieces. Toss the shredded brisket in the pan juices to coat.
3. Assemble the Tacos: Warm the tortillas in a dry skillet or microwave. Place a spoonful of shredded brisket onto each tortilla. Top with shredded lettuce or cabbage, diced tomatoes, diced red onion, and chopped fresh cilantro. Squeeze lime juice over the top.
4. Serve: Serve the BBQ brisket tacos immediately, with lime wedges on the side for squeezing and additional barbecue sauce for drizzling, if desired.
5. Enjoy: Enjoy these BBQ brisket tacos as a delicious and satisfying meal!

These BBQ brisket tacos are bursting with flavor and make for a hearty and satisfying meal. They're perfect for a casual dinner or a gathering with friends and family!

Spicy Chicken Wings

Ingredients:

For the Chicken Wings:

- 2 lbs chicken wings, split into drumettes and flats
- Salt and pepper, to taste
- 1 tablespoon vegetable oil

For the Spicy Sauce:

- 1/2 cup hot sauce (such as Frank's RedHot)
- 1/4 cup melted butter
- 2 tablespoons honey or maple syrup
- 1 tablespoon apple cider vinegar
- 1 teaspoon garlic powder
- 1/2 teaspoon smoked paprika
- 1/2 teaspoon cayenne pepper (adjust to taste for desired spice level)
- Ranch or blue cheese dressing, for serving
- Celery sticks, for serving

Instructions:

1. Preheat the Oven: Preheat your oven to 400°F (200°C).
2. Prepare the Chicken Wings: Pat the chicken wings dry with paper towels and season with salt and pepper. Place the seasoned wings in a large bowl and drizzle with vegetable oil. Toss to coat evenly.
3. Bake the Chicken Wings: Arrange the chicken wings in a single layer on a baking sheet lined with parchment paper or aluminum foil. Bake in the preheated oven for 40-45 minutes, turning halfway through, or until the wings are golden brown and crispy.
4. Make the Spicy Sauce: In a small saucepan, combine hot sauce, melted butter, honey or maple syrup, apple cider vinegar, garlic powder, smoked paprika, and cayenne pepper. Bring the mixture to a simmer over medium heat, stirring occasionally. Remove from heat.
5. Coat the Wings: Transfer the baked chicken wings to a large bowl. Pour the spicy sauce over the wings and toss to coat evenly.
6. Serve: Serve the spicy chicken wings hot, with ranch or blue cheese dressing for dipping and celery sticks on the side.

7. Enjoy: Enjoy these spicy chicken wings as a delicious appetizer or main dish for game day or any casual gathering!

These spicy chicken wings are crispy on the outside, juicy on the inside, and packed with flavor from the tangy and spicy sauce. They're sure to be a hit at any party or gathering! Adjust the level of cayenne pepper to suit your taste preferences for spice.

Italian Meatball Subs

Ingredients:

For the Meatballs:

- 1 lb ground beef
- 1/2 lb ground pork
- 1/2 cup breadcrumbs
- 1/4 cup grated Parmesan cheese
- 1/4 cup chopped fresh parsley
- 1 egg
- 2 cloves garlic, minced
- 1 teaspoon dried oregano
- 1 teaspoon dried basil
- Salt and pepper, to taste

For the Marinara Sauce:

- 2 tablespoons olive oil
- 1 small onion, diced
- 2 cloves garlic, minced
- 1 can (28 oz) crushed tomatoes
- 1 teaspoon dried oregano
- 1 teaspoon dried basil
- Salt and pepper, to taste

For the Subs:

- 4-6 sub rolls or hoagie buns
- 1 cup shredded mozzarella cheese
- Chopped fresh parsley, for garnish (optional)

Instructions:

1. Prepare the Meatballs: In a large mixing bowl, combine the ground beef, ground pork, breadcrumbs, grated Parmesan cheese, chopped parsley, egg, minced garlic, dried oregano, dried basil, salt, and pepper. Use your hands to mix until well combined. Shape the mixture into meatballs, about 1-2 inches in diameter.
2. Cook the Meatballs: Heat a large skillet over medium heat. Add a drizzle of olive oil to the skillet. Working in batches, add the meatballs to the skillet and cook

until browned on all sides and cooked through, about 8-10 minutes. Transfer the cooked meatballs to a plate and set aside.
3. Prepare the Marinara Sauce: In the same skillet, heat olive oil over medium heat. Add diced onion and minced garlic, and cook until softened and fragrant, about 3-4 minutes. Stir in crushed tomatoes, dried oregano, dried basil, salt, and pepper. Bring the sauce to a simmer and let it cook for 10-15 minutes, stirring occasionally.
4. Assemble the Subs: Preheat your oven to 375°F (190°C). Slice the sub rolls or hoagie buns in half lengthwise, without cutting all the way through. Place the cooked meatballs in the marinara sauce and let them simmer for a few minutes to absorb the flavors. Spoon the meatballs and marinara sauce onto the bottom halves of the sub rolls. Sprinkle shredded mozzarella cheese over the meatballs.
5. Bake the Subs: Place the assembled subs on a baking sheet and transfer to the preheated oven. Bake for 10-15 minutes, or until the cheese is melted and bubbly.
6. Garnish and Serve: Remove the subs from the oven and garnish with chopped fresh parsley, if desired. Serve the Italian meatball subs hot, and enjoy!

These Italian meatball subs are hearty, flavorful, and perfect for a satisfying meal. Serve them for lunch, dinner, or as a crowd-pleasing option for game day gatherings or casual get-togethers!

Vietnamese Banh Mi Sandwiches

Ingredients:

For the Marinated Pork:

- 1 lb pork tenderloin or pork loin, thinly sliced
- 3 tablespoons soy sauce
- 2 tablespoons fish sauce
- 2 tablespoons brown sugar
- 2 cloves garlic, minced
- 1 teaspoon five-spice powder
- 1 tablespoon vegetable oil

For the Pickled Vegetables:

- 1 carrot, julienned
- 1 daikon radish, julienned
- 1/4 cup rice vinegar
- 2 tablespoons sugar
- 1/2 teaspoon salt

For the Sandwiches:

- 4-6 French baguettes or sandwich rolls
- Mayonnaise
- Fresh cilantro leaves
- Thinly sliced cucumber
- Thinly sliced jalapeño peppers (optional)
- Sriracha or chili sauce (optional)

Instructions:

1. Marinate the Pork: In a bowl, combine soy sauce, fish sauce, brown sugar, minced garlic, five-spice powder, and vegetable oil. Add the thinly sliced pork and toss to coat evenly. Cover and marinate in the refrigerator for at least 30 minutes, or up to 2 hours.
2. Prepare the Pickled Vegetables: In a separate bowl, combine julienned carrot and daikon radish with rice vinegar, sugar, and salt. Toss to coat evenly. Let the vegetables pickle in the refrigerator for at least 30 minutes, or up to 2 hours.

3. Cook the Pork: Heat a skillet or grill pan over medium-high heat. Add the marinated pork slices in a single layer and cook for 2-3 minutes per side, or until browned and cooked through. Remove from heat and set aside.
4. Assemble the Sandwiches: Slice the French baguettes or sandwich rolls in half lengthwise. Spread mayonnaise on one side of each bread roll. Layer the cooked pork slices, pickled vegetables, fresh cilantro leaves, thinly sliced cucumber, and thinly sliced jalapeño peppers (if using) on top.
5. Optional: Drizzle Sriracha or chili sauce over the fillings for extra heat, if desired.
6. Serve: Serve the Vietnamese banh mi sandwiches immediately, and enjoy!

These Vietnamese banh mi sandwiches are a delightful fusion of flavors and textures, with savory marinated pork, tangy pickled vegetables, creamy mayonnaise, fresh herbs, and crunchy bread. They're perfect for lunch, dinner, or anytime you're craving a tasty and satisfying sandwich!

Breakfast Burritos

Ingredients:

- 6 large eggs
- 1/4 cup milk
- Salt and pepper, to taste
- 1 tablespoon vegetable oil
- 1 bell pepper, diced
- 1 small onion, diced
- 1 cup diced cooked ham or cooked crumbled sausage
- 1 cup shredded cheddar cheese
- 4 large flour tortillas
- Salsa, for serving (optional)
- Sour cream, for serving (optional)
- Avocado slices, for serving (optional)

Instructions:

1. Prepare the Egg Mixture: In a bowl, whisk together the eggs, milk, salt, and pepper until well combined.
2. Cook the Eggs: Heat vegetable oil in a large skillet over medium heat. Add diced bell pepper and onion to the skillet and cook until softened, about 5 minutes. Pour the egg mixture into the skillet and cook, stirring occasionally, until the eggs are scrambled and cooked through. Add the diced cooked ham or crumbled sausage to the skillet and stir to combine. Remove from heat.
3. Assemble the Burritos: Warm the flour tortillas in the microwave for a few seconds to make them pliable. Divide the scrambled egg mixture evenly among the tortillas, placing it in the center of each tortilla. Sprinkle shredded cheddar cheese over the egg mixture.
4. Roll the Burritos: Fold the sides of each tortilla over the filling, then roll up tightly from the bottom to form a burrito.
5. Optional: If desired, wrap each burrito individually in aluminum foil for easier handling and transport.
6. Serve: Serve the breakfast burritos immediately, with salsa, sour cream, and avocado slices on the side for dipping or topping, if desired.
7. Enjoy: Enjoy these hearty and flavorful breakfast burritos as a delicious way to start your day!

These breakfast burritos are versatile and customizable, making them perfect for busy mornings or a leisurely weekend brunch. Feel free to add other fillings such as diced tomatoes, cooked potatoes, black beans, or spinach to suit your taste preferences.

Cajun Crawfish Boil

Ingredients:

- 5-10 lbs live crawfish
- 6-8 quarts water
- 2 cups Cajun seafood boil seasoning (such as Zatarain's or Old Bay)
- 2 lbs small red potatoes
- 4 ears corn on the cob, shucked and halved
- 2 lbs smoked sausage or andouille sausage, cut into chunks
- 2 onions, quartered
- 4 cloves garlic, smashed
- 2 lemons, halved
- Cajun seasoning or hot sauce, for serving (optional)
- Melted butter, for serving (optional)

Instructions:

1. Prepare the Crawfish: Rinse the live crawfish under cold water to remove any dirt or debris. Discard any dead crawfish or ones with broken shells.
2. Boil Water: Fill a large stockpot with 6-8 quarts of water and bring it to a rolling boil over high heat.
3. Add Seasoning: Once the water is boiling, add the Cajun seafood boil seasoning to the pot. Stir to dissolve the seasoning into the water.
4. Boil Potatoes: Add the small red potatoes to the boiling water. Cook for 10-12 minutes, or until the potatoes are just tender.
5. Add Other Ingredients: Add the halved corn on the cob, chunks of smoked sausage or andouille sausage, quartered onions, smashed garlic cloves, and halved lemons to the pot. Let the mixture return to a boil.
6. Cook Crawfish: Carefully add the live crawfish to the pot. Cover the pot and let the crawfish boil for 5-7 minutes, or until they turn bright red and float to the surface. Be careful not to overcook the crawfish, as they can become tough.
7. Drain and Serve: Once the crawfish are cooked, turn off the heat and carefully drain the contents of the pot into a large colander or outdoor table covered with newspapers. Let the excess water drain off.
8. Serve: Transfer the boiled crawfish, potatoes, corn, sausage, onions, and garlic to a large serving platter or dump them directly onto the newspaper-covered table. Serve hot with Cajun seasoning or hot sauce and melted butter on the side for dipping.
9. Enjoy: Dig in and enjoy this delicious Cajun crawfish boil with friends and family!

This Cajun crawfish boil is a classic Southern dish that's perfect for gatherings, backyard cookouts, or any casual occasion. Be sure to have plenty of napkins and cold drinks on hand, as things might get messy and spicy!

Beef Bulgogi Tacos

Ingredients:

For the Beef Bulgogi:

- 1 lb beef sirloin or ribeye, thinly sliced
- 1/4 cup soy sauce
- 2 tablespoons brown sugar
- 2 tablespoons sesame oil
- 2 cloves garlic, minced
- 1 teaspoon grated ginger
- 1 tablespoon rice vinegar
- 1 tablespoon sesame seeds
- 2 green onions, chopped
- 1 tablespoon vegetable oil, for cooking

For the Tacos:

- 8-10 small flour or corn tortillas
- 1 cup shredded lettuce or cabbage
- 1/2 cup sliced cucumber
- 1/2 cup shredded carrots
- 1/4 cup sliced radishes
- Fresh cilantro leaves, for garnish
- Lime wedges, for serving

Instructions:

1. Marinate the Beef: In a bowl, whisk together soy sauce, brown sugar, sesame oil, minced garlic, grated ginger, rice vinegar, sesame seeds, and chopped green onions. Add the thinly sliced beef to the marinade and toss to coat. Cover and refrigerate for at least 1 hour, or up to overnight.
2. Cook the Beef: Heat vegetable oil in a large skillet or grill pan over medium-high heat. Add the marinated beef slices in a single layer and cook for 2-3 minutes per side, or until browned and cooked through. Remove from heat and set aside.
3. Prepare the Toppings: In the meantime, prepare the taco toppings. Shred lettuce or cabbage, slice cucumber, shred carrots, and slice radishes. Arrange the toppings on a serving platter.
4. Warm the Tortillas: Heat the tortillas in a dry skillet or microwave until warm and pliable.

5. Assemble the Tacos: Place a spoonful of cooked beef bulgogi onto each warm tortilla. Top with shredded lettuce or cabbage, sliced cucumber, shredded carrots, and sliced radishes. Garnish with fresh cilantro leaves.
6. Serve: Serve the beef bulgogi tacos immediately, with lime wedges on the side for squeezing.
7. Enjoy: Enjoy these delicious beef bulgogi tacos as a flavorful and satisfying meal!

These beef bulgogi tacos are a fusion of Korean and Mexican flavors, with tender marinated beef, crisp vegetables, and fresh herbs, all wrapped in warm tortillas. They're perfect for a casual dinner or a fun meal with friends and family!

Indian Butter Chicken Wraps

Ingredients:

For the Butter Chicken:

- 1 lb boneless, skinless chicken breasts, cut into bite-sized pieces
- 1/4 cup plain yogurt
- 2 tablespoons lemon juice
- 2 cloves garlic, minced
- 1 tablespoon grated ginger
- 1 teaspoon ground cumin
- 1 teaspoon ground coriander
- 1 teaspoon garam masala
- 1/2 teaspoon turmeric powder
- 1/4 teaspoon cayenne pepper (optional, for extra heat)
- Salt and pepper, to taste
- 2 tablespoons butter
- 1 onion, finely chopped
- 1 can (14 oz) crushed tomatoes
- 1/2 cup heavy cream
- Fresh cilantro leaves, for garnish

For the Wraps:

- 4-6 large flour tortillas or naan bread
- Shredded lettuce or cabbage
- Sliced cucumber
- Sliced red onion
- Plain yogurt or raita
- Mango chutney or tamarind sauce (optional)

Instructions:

1. Marinate the Chicken: In a bowl, combine plain yogurt, lemon juice, minced garlic, grated ginger, ground cumin, ground coriander, garam masala, turmeric powder, cayenne pepper (if using), salt, and pepper. Add the bite-sized chicken pieces to the marinade and toss to coat. Cover and refrigerate for at least 30 minutes, or up to overnight.
2. Cook the Butter Chicken: In a large skillet or saucepan, melt butter over medium heat. Add finely chopped onion and cook until softened and translucent, about 5

minutes. Add the marinated chicken pieces and cook until browned on all sides, about 5-7 minutes.
3. Simmer the Sauce: Stir in crushed tomatoes and bring the mixture to a simmer. Reduce heat to low and let the sauce simmer for 15-20 minutes, stirring occasionally, until the chicken is cooked through and the sauce has thickened. Stir in heavy cream and simmer for an additional 5 minutes.
4. Assemble the Wraps: Warm the flour tortillas or naan bread. Place a spoonful of butter chicken onto each tortilla or naan bread. Top with shredded lettuce or cabbage, sliced cucumber, sliced red onion, and a dollop of plain yogurt or raita. Drizzle with mango chutney or tamarind sauce, if using. Garnish with fresh cilantro leaves.
5. Roll Up the Wraps: Fold the sides of each tortilla or naan bread over the filling, then roll up tightly from the bottom to form a wrap.
6. Serve: Serve the Indian Butter Chicken Wraps immediately, and enjoy!

These Indian Butter Chicken Wraps are packed with flavorful and aromatic butter chicken, crisp vegetables, and creamy yogurt, all wrapped up in warm tortillas or naan bread. They're perfect for a quick and satisfying meal that's bursting with Indian-inspired flavors!

Classic Cheeseburgers

Ingredients:

For the Burgers:

- 1 lb ground beef (80/20 blend recommended)
- Salt and pepper, to taste
- 4 hamburger buns
- 4 slices cheese (such as American, cheddar, or Swiss)
- Lettuce leaves
- Sliced tomatoes
- Sliced onions
- Pickles (optional)

For the Burger Sauce:

- 1/4 cup mayonnaise
- 1 tablespoon ketchup
- 1 tablespoon mustard
- 1 teaspoon pickle relish
- Salt and pepper, to taste

Instructions:

1. Preheat the Grill or Skillet: Preheat your grill or skillet over medium-high heat.
2. Form the Patties: Divide the ground beef into 4 equal portions and shape each portion into a patty, about 1/2 inch thick. Season both sides of the patties with salt and pepper.
3. Cook the Patties: Place the burger patties on the preheated grill or skillet. Cook for 4-5 minutes on one side, then flip and cook for an additional 4-5 minutes on the other side, or until the patties reach your desired level of doneness. During the last minute of cooking, place a slice of cheese on top of each patty to melt.
4. Toast the Buns: While the patties are cooking, split the hamburger buns and lightly toast them on the grill or skillet.
5. Prepare the Burger Sauce: In a small bowl, mix together mayonnaise, ketchup, mustard, pickle relish, salt, and pepper to make the burger sauce.
6. Assemble the Burgers: Spread a dollop of burger sauce on the bottom half of each toasted bun. Place a cooked cheeseburger patty on top of the sauce. Add lettuce leaves, sliced tomatoes, sliced onions, and pickles (if using). Top with the other half of the bun.

7. Serve: Serve the classic cheeseburgers immediately, and enjoy!

These classic cheeseburgers are simple, delicious, and perfect for a backyard barbecue or weeknight dinner. Customize them with your favorite toppings and enjoy the timeless combination of juicy beef, melted cheese, and flavorful burger sauce!

Buffalo Cauliflower Bites

Ingredients:

For the Cauliflower Bites:

- 1 head cauliflower, cut into bite-sized florets
- 1 cup all-purpose flour (or chickpea flour for gluten-free option)
- 1 cup water
- 1 teaspoon garlic powder
- 1/2 teaspoon paprika
- Salt and pepper, to taste
- Cooking spray or olive oil

For the Buffalo Sauce:

- 1/4 cup hot sauce (such as Frank's RedHot)
- 2 tablespoons unsalted butter (or vegan butter for vegan option)
- 1 tablespoon honey (or maple syrup for vegan option)
- 1 teaspoon apple cider vinegar
- 1/2 teaspoon garlic powder
- Salt, to taste

Instructions:

1. Preheat the Oven: Preheat your oven to 450°F (230°C). Line a baking sheet with parchment paper or lightly grease it with cooking spray or olive oil.
2. Prepare the Cauliflower Bites: In a large bowl, whisk together flour, water, garlic powder, paprika, salt, and pepper until smooth and well combined. Add cauliflower florets to the bowl and toss until evenly coated.
3. Bake the Cauliflower Bites: Spread the coated cauliflower florets in a single layer on the prepared baking sheet. Bake in the preheated oven for 20-25 minutes, flipping halfway through, or until the cauliflower is golden brown and crispy.
4. Make the Buffalo Sauce: In a small saucepan, melt butter over low heat. Stir in hot sauce, honey (or maple syrup), apple cider vinegar, garlic powder, and salt. Cook for 1-2 minutes, stirring constantly, until the sauce is heated through and well combined.
5. Coat the Cauliflower: Once the cauliflower bites are crispy and golden brown, remove them from the oven and transfer them to a large bowl. Pour the prepared buffalo sauce over the cauliflower bites and toss until evenly coated.

6. Serve: Transfer the buffalo cauliflower bites to a serving platter and serve hot. Enjoy with ranch or blue cheese dressing and celery sticks on the side!

These buffalo cauliflower bites are crispy, spicy, and addictive, making them a perfect appetizer or snack for game day gatherings, parties, or movie nights. They're also a tasty vegetarian or vegan alternative to traditional buffalo wings! Adjust the amount of hot sauce to suit your spice preference.

Cuban Mojo Pork Tacos

Ingredients:

For the Mojo Pork:

- 2 lbs pork shoulder or pork butt, trimmed of excess fat and cut into chunks
- 1/2 cup orange juice
- 1/4 cup lime juice
- 1/4 cup olive oil
- 6 cloves garlic, minced
- 1 tablespoon fresh oregano leaves, chopped
- 1 teaspoon ground cumin
- 1 teaspoon smoked paprika
- Salt and pepper, to taste

For the Tacos:

- 8-10 small corn or flour tortillas
- 1 cup shredded cabbage or lettuce
- 1 cup diced fresh pineapple
- 1/2 cup diced red onion
- 1/4 cup chopped fresh cilantro
- Lime wedges, for serving

Instructions:

1. Marinate the Pork: In a large bowl or resealable plastic bag, combine orange juice, lime juice, olive oil, minced garlic, chopped oregano, ground cumin, smoked paprika, salt, and pepper. Add the pork chunks to the marinade and toss to coat. Cover and refrigerate for at least 4 hours, or overnight, to marinate.
2. Preheat the Grill or Oven: Preheat your grill to medium-high heat or preheat your oven to 350°F (175°C).
3. Cook the Pork: If grilling, remove the pork from the marinade and grill over medium-high heat for 4-5 minutes per side, or until the pork is cooked through and caramelized. If using the oven, transfer the pork and marinade to a baking dish and bake for 1-1.5 hours, or until the pork is tender and cooked through.
4. Shred the Pork: Once the pork is cooked, transfer it to a cutting board and shred it using two forks.

5. Assemble the Tacos: Warm the tortillas in a dry skillet or microwave. Fill each tortilla with shredded mojo pork, shredded cabbage or lettuce, diced pineapple, diced red onion, and chopped cilantro.
6. Serve: Serve the Cuban Mojo Pork Tacos immediately, with lime wedges on the side for squeezing.
7. Enjoy: Enjoy these flavorful and vibrant Cuban Mojo Pork Tacos as a delicious and satisfying meal!

These Cuban Mojo Pork Tacos are bursting with citrusy, garlicky flavors and are perfect for a festive dinner or a summer barbecue. The combination of tender shredded pork, sweet pineapple, and tangy red onion makes for a delicious taco filling that's sure to impress!

Southern Fried Chicken Sandwiches

Ingredients:

For the Fried Chicken:

- 4 boneless, skinless chicken breasts
- 1 cup buttermilk
- 1 cup all-purpose flour
- 1 teaspoon paprika
- 1 teaspoon garlic powder
- 1 teaspoon onion powder
- 1/2 teaspoon cayenne pepper (optional, for extra heat)
- Salt and pepper, to taste
- Vegetable oil, for frying

For the Sandwiches:

- 4 hamburger buns or brioche buns
- Mayonnaise
- Pickle slices
- Lettuce leaves
- Sliced tomatoes
- Sliced red onion (optional)

Instructions:

1. Prepare the Chicken: Place the chicken breasts between two sheets of plastic wrap and gently pound them to an even thickness, about 1/2 inch thick. Season both sides of the chicken breasts with salt and pepper.
2. Marinate the Chicken: In a shallow dish, pour the buttermilk over the chicken breasts, ensuring they are fully submerged. Cover and refrigerate for at least 1 hour, or up to overnight, to marinate.
3. Prepare the Coating: In another shallow dish, whisk together the all-purpose flour, paprika, garlic powder, onion powder, cayenne pepper (if using), salt, and pepper.
4. Coat the Chicken: Remove the marinated chicken breasts from the buttermilk, allowing any excess buttermilk to drip off. Dredge the chicken breasts in the seasoned flour mixture, pressing down firmly to coat both sides evenly. Shake off any excess flour.
5. Fry the Chicken: In a large skillet or deep fryer, heat vegetable oil to 350°F (175°C). Carefully add the coated chicken breasts to the hot oil and fry for 6-8

minutes per side, or until golden brown and cooked through. The internal temperature of the chicken should reach 165°F (75°C). Drain the fried chicken on a wire rack or paper towels to remove excess oil.
6. Assemble the Sandwiches: Spread mayonnaise on the bottom half of each hamburger bun or brioche bun. Place a fried chicken breast on top of the mayonnaise. Top with pickle slices, lettuce leaves, sliced tomatoes, and sliced red onion (if using). Cover with the top half of the bun.
7. Serve: Serve the Southern Fried Chicken Sandwiches immediately, and enjoy!

These Southern Fried Chicken Sandwiches are crispy, juicy, and packed with flavor. Serve them alongside your favorite side dishes, such as coleslaw, potato salad, or french fries, for a delicious and satisfying meal that's perfect for lunch or dinner!

Japanese Ramen Noodle Soup

Ingredients:

For the Broth:

- 8 cups chicken broth or vegetable broth
- 4 cloves garlic, minced
- 2-inch piece of ginger, peeled and sliced
- 1 onion, quartered
- 2 tablespoons soy sauce
- 1 tablespoon mirin (Japanese rice wine) or rice vinegar
- 1 tablespoon miso paste (white or red)
- 1 tablespoon sesame oil
- Salt and pepper, to taste

For the Ramen:

- 4 packs of ramen noodles (about 8 ounces total)
- 4 eggs
- 2 cups sliced cooked chicken, pork, or tofu
- 2 cups baby spinach or bok choy leaves
- 1 cup sliced mushrooms (shiitake, cremini, or button)
- 4 green onions, thinly sliced
- Nori sheets, for garnish (optional)
- Sesame seeds, for garnish (optional)

Instructions:

1. Prepare the Broth: In a large pot, combine chicken broth or vegetable broth, minced garlic, sliced ginger, quartered onion, soy sauce, mirin or rice vinegar, miso paste, sesame oil, salt, and pepper. Bring the mixture to a boil, then reduce heat to low and simmer for 20-30 minutes to allow the flavors to develop. Strain the broth through a fine mesh sieve and discard the solids. Return the strained broth to the pot and keep warm over low heat.
2. Prepare the Eggs: Bring a separate pot of water to a boil. Carefully add the eggs to the boiling water and cook for 6-7 minutes for soft-boiled eggs or 10-12 minutes for hard-boiled eggs. Transfer the cooked eggs to a bowl of ice water to cool. Once cool, peel the eggs and slice them in half lengthwise.

3. Cook the Ramen Noodles: Cook the ramen noodles according to the package instructions. Drain and rinse the cooked noodles under cold water to stop the cooking process and prevent them from sticking together.
4. Assemble the Ramen Bowls: Divide the cooked ramen noodles among four serving bowls. Ladle the hot broth over the noodles, making sure to distribute the solids evenly. Top each bowl with sliced cooked chicken, pork, or tofu, baby spinach or bok choy leaves, sliced mushrooms, and green onions. Add a soft-boiled or hard-boiled egg half to each bowl.
5. Garnish and Serve: Garnish the ramen bowls with nori sheets and sesame seeds, if desired. Serve the Japanese Ramen Noodle Soup hot and enjoy!

This Japanese Ramen Noodle Soup is comforting, flavorful, and fully customizable with your favorite toppings. Feel free to add additional ingredients such as corn kernels, bamboo shoots, bean sprouts, or sliced jalapeños to suit your taste preferences. Enjoy this delicious and satisfying meal for lunch or dinner!

Philly Cheesesteak Egg Rolls

Ingredients:

- 1 lb thinly sliced ribeye steak
- 1 tablespoon vegetable oil
- 1 onion, thinly sliced
- 1 green bell pepper, thinly sliced
- 8-10 egg roll wrappers
- 8-10 slices provolone cheese
- Salt and pepper, to taste
- Vegetable oil, for frying
- Ketchup or your favorite dipping sauce, for serving

Instructions:

1. Prepare the Filling: In a large skillet, heat 1 tablespoon of vegetable oil over medium-high heat. Add the thinly sliced ribeye steak to the skillet and cook for 2-3 minutes, stirring occasionally, until browned and cooked through. Remove the steak from the skillet and set aside.
2. In the same skillet, add the thinly sliced onion and green bell pepper. Cook for 3-4 minutes, stirring occasionally, until the vegetables are softened and slightly caramelized. Season with salt and pepper, to taste. Remove from heat and set aside.
3. Assemble the Egg Rolls: Lay an egg roll wrapper on a clean surface with one corner pointing towards you. Place a slice of provolone cheese diagonally across the center of the wrapper. Spoon a portion of the cooked steak and sautéed vegetables on top of the cheese.
4. Fold the bottom corner of the wrapper over the filling, then fold in the sides, and roll tightly towards the top corner, sealing the edges with a little water. Repeat with the remaining wrappers and filling.
5. Fry the Egg Rolls: In a large skillet or deep fryer, heat vegetable oil to 350°F (175°C). Carefully add the egg rolls to the hot oil, a few at a time, and fry for 3-4 minutes, or until golden brown and crispy. Use tongs to remove the egg rolls from the oil and drain on paper towels.
6. Serve: Serve the Philly Cheesesteak Egg Rolls hot, with ketchup or your favorite dipping sauce on the side.

These Philly Cheesesteak Egg Rolls are a delicious twist on the classic sandwich, with tender steak, sautéed onions, and bell peppers, all wrapped up in a crispy egg roll wrapper. They make a fantastic appetizer or snack for parties, game days, or any occasion!

Pulled Pork Mac and Cheese

Ingredients:

- 8 ounces elbow macaroni
- 2 cups pulled pork (homemade or store-bought)
- 2 tablespoons butter
- 2 tablespoons all-purpose flour
- 2 cups milk
- 2 cups shredded cheddar cheese
- 1 cup shredded mozzarella cheese
- Salt and pepper, to taste
- Optional toppings: chopped green onions, crispy bacon bits

Instructions:

1. Preheat your oven to 375°F (190°C). Grease a 9x13-inch baking dish and set aside.
2. Cook the elbow macaroni according to the package instructions until al dente. Drain and set aside.
3. In a large saucepan, melt the butter over medium heat. Stir in the flour and cook for 1-2 minutes until the mixture turns golden brown and bubbly.
4. Gradually whisk in the milk, stirring constantly to prevent lumps from forming. Cook until the mixture thickens, about 5 minutes.
5. Reduce the heat to low and add the shredded cheddar cheese and shredded mozzarella cheese to the saucepan. Stir until the cheese is melted and the sauce is smooth. Season with salt and pepper to taste.
6. Add the cooked elbow macaroni and pulled pork to the cheese sauce, stirring until well combined.
7. Pour the mac and cheese mixture into the prepared baking dish, spreading it out evenly.
8. Bake in the preheated oven for 20-25 minutes, or until the top is golden brown and bubbly.
9. Remove from the oven and let it cool slightly before serving.
10. Garnish with chopped green onions or crispy bacon bits if desired.
11. Serve hot and enjoy your delicious Pulled Pork Mac and Cheese!

This hearty and flavorful dish combines the creamy comfort of mac and cheese with the rich taste of pulled pork, creating a satisfying meal that's perfect for any occasion.

Vegetarian Falafel Wraps

Ingredients:

For the Falafel:

- 1 can (15 oz) chickpeas, drained and rinsed
- 1/2 cup chopped fresh parsley
- 1/4 cup chopped fresh cilantro
- 1/4 cup chopped red onion
- 2 cloves garlic, minced
- 2 tablespoons all-purpose flour or chickpea flour
- 1 teaspoon ground cumin
- 1 teaspoon ground coriander
- 1/2 teaspoon baking powder
- Salt and pepper, to taste
- Vegetable oil, for frying

For the Yogurt Sauce:

- 1 cup Greek yogurt
- 1 tablespoon lemon juice
- 1 tablespoon tahini
- 1 clove garlic, minced
- Salt and pepper, to taste

For the Wraps:

- 4 large whole wheat or spinach wraps
- 2 cups shredded lettuce or cabbage
- 1 cucumber, thinly sliced
- 1 tomato, diced
- 1/2 red onion, thinly sliced
- Pickled turnips (optional)
- Fresh mint leaves (optional)
- Hot sauce (optional)

Instructions:

1. Prepare the Falafel: In a food processor, combine the chickpeas, parsley, cilantro, red onion, garlic, flour, cumin, coriander, baking powder, salt, and pepper. Pulse

until the mixture comes together but is still slightly coarse. You may need to scrape down the sides of the bowl occasionally.
2. Shape the falafel mixture into small patties or balls using your hands. Place them on a baking sheet lined with parchment paper.
3. Heat vegetable oil in a large skillet over medium heat. Fry the falafel in batches until golden brown and crispy, about 3-4 minutes per side. Transfer to a plate lined with paper towels to drain excess oil.
4. Prepare the Yogurt Sauce: In a small bowl, whisk together Greek yogurt, lemon juice, tahini, minced garlic, salt, and pepper until smooth and well combined. Adjust seasoning to taste.
5. Assemble the Wraps: Lay out the wraps on a clean surface. Spread a generous spoonful of yogurt sauce onto each wrap.
6. Divide the shredded lettuce or cabbage, cucumber slices, diced tomato, and thinly sliced red onion among the wraps. Add a few falafel patties on top of the vegetables.
7. If desired, add pickled turnips, fresh mint leaves, and a drizzle of hot sauce for extra flavor.
8. Wrap it Up: Fold the bottom edge of each wrap up and over the filling, then fold in the sides, and roll tightly towards the top to seal.
9. Serve: Serve the Vegetarian Falafel Wraps immediately, or wrap them in foil for a portable lunch or picnic.

Enjoy these flavorful and satisfying Vegetarian Falafel Wraps as a delicious and nutritious meal option!

Hawaiian Poke Bowls

Ingredients:

For the Poke:

- 1 lb sushi-grade ahi tuna, cubed
- 1/4 cup soy sauce
- 1 tablespoon sesame oil
- 1 tablespoon rice vinegar
- 1 teaspoon sriracha sauce (optional)
- 1 teaspoon honey or sugar
- 2 green onions, thinly sliced
- 1 teaspoon sesame seeds
- 1 avocado, diced (optional)
- 1/2 cucumber, thinly sliced
- Cooked sushi rice or brown rice, for serving

For the Garnish:

- Thinly sliced radishes
- Sliced jalapeños
- Sliced mango or pineapple
- Edamame beans
- Seaweed salad
- Pickled ginger
- Furikake (Japanese seasoning blend)

Instructions:

1. Prepare the Poke: In a medium bowl, combine the cubed ahi tuna, soy sauce, sesame oil, rice vinegar, sriracha sauce (if using), and honey or sugar. Toss gently to coat the tuna evenly. Cover and refrigerate for at least 15-20 minutes to allow the flavors to meld.
2. Cook the Rice: While the tuna is marinating, cook sushi rice or brown rice according to the package instructions. Once cooked, let it cool slightly.
3. Assemble the Poke Bowls: Divide the cooked rice among serving bowls. Top each bowl with a portion of the marinated tuna. Arrange diced avocado, sliced cucumber, thinly sliced radishes, sliced jalapeños, sliced mango or pineapple, edamame beans, seaweed salad, and pickled ginger around the tuna.

4. Garnish and Serve: Sprinkle each bowl with sliced green onions, sesame seeds, and furikake. Serve the Hawaiian Poke Bowls immediately, with additional soy sauce or sriracha sauce on the side if desired.
5. Enjoy: Mix the ingredients together and enjoy your delicious Hawaiian Poke Bowls!

These Hawaiian Poke Bowls are fresh, flavorful, and customizable to your taste preferences. Feel free to add or substitute ingredients based on what you have on hand or your personal preferences. They make a nutritious and satisfying meal option for lunch or dinner!

Korean Kimchi Fries

Ingredients:

For the Fries:

- 1 lb frozen French fries or homemade fries
- Vegetable oil, for frying (if making homemade fries)

For the Kimchi Topping:

- 1 cup kimchi, chopped
- 1 tablespoon sesame oil
- 2 green onions, thinly sliced
- 1 tablespoon sesame seeds
- 1 tablespoon gochujang (Korean chili paste)
- 1 tablespoon soy sauce
- 1 teaspoon honey or sugar
- 1 clove garlic, minced

For the Garnish:

- 1/2 cup shredded mozzarella cheese
- 1/4 cup mayonnaise
- 1 tablespoon sriracha sauce
- 1 tablespoon chopped fresh cilantro
- 1 tablespoon chopped green onions
- Toasted sesame seeds, for garnish
- Sliced fresh red chili (optional, for extra heat)

Instructions:

1. Prepare the Fries: If using frozen French fries, cook them according to the package instructions until crispy and golden brown. If making homemade fries, cut potatoes into fries, rinse under cold water, and pat dry. Heat vegetable oil in a deep fryer or large pot to 350°F (175°C). Fry the potato fries in batches until golden and crispy, about 3-4 minutes per batch. Drain on paper towels and season with salt.
2. Make the Kimchi Topping: In a skillet, heat sesame oil over medium heat. Add chopped kimchi and cook for 2-3 minutes until slightly softened. Stir in green onions, sesame seeds, gochujang, soy sauce, honey or sugar, and minced garlic.

Cook for another 2-3 minutes, stirring occasionally, until the flavors are combined and the sauce thickens slightly. Remove from heat.

3. Assemble the Kimchi Fries: Arrange the cooked fries on a large serving platter or individual plates. Spoon the cooked kimchi mixture over the fries. Sprinkle shredded mozzarella cheese over the top.
4. Make the Spicy Mayo: In a small bowl, mix together mayonnaise and sriracha sauce until well combined. Drizzle the spicy mayo over the kimchi fries.
5. Garnish and Serve: Sprinkle chopped fresh cilantro, green onions, and toasted sesame seeds over the top of the fries. If desired, add sliced fresh red chili for extra heat. Serve the Korean Kimchi Fries immediately while hot.

Enjoy these Korean Kimchi Fries as a delicious and flavorful appetizer or snack! They're perfect for sharing with friends and family at gatherings or game nights. Adjust the amount of sriracha sauce to suit your spice preference.

Chicken Shawarma Pitas

Ingredients:

For the Chicken Shawarma:

- 1 lb boneless, skinless chicken thighs, thinly sliced
- 2 cloves garlic, minced
- 1 teaspoon ground cumin
- 1 teaspoon ground paprika
- 1 teaspoon ground turmeric
- 1/2 teaspoon ground cinnamon
- 1/4 teaspoon ground cloves
- 1/4 teaspoon cayenne pepper
- 2 tablespoons lemon juice
- 2 tablespoons olive oil
- Salt and pepper, to taste

For the Yogurt Sauce:

- 1 cup Greek yogurt
- 2 tablespoons lemon juice
- 1 tablespoon tahini
- 1 clove garlic, minced
- 1 tablespoon chopped fresh parsley
- Salt and pepper, to taste

For Serving:

- 4 pita bread rounds
- Sliced tomatoes
- Sliced cucumbers
- Thinly sliced red onion
- Chopped fresh parsley or cilantro
- Pickles (optional)

Instructions:

1. Marinate the Chicken: In a bowl, combine the sliced chicken thighs, minced garlic, ground cumin, ground paprika, ground turmeric, ground cinnamon, ground cloves, cayenne pepper, lemon juice, olive oil, salt, and pepper. Toss well to coat the

chicken evenly in the marinade. Cover and refrigerate for at least 30 minutes, or up to overnight.
2. Prepare the Yogurt Sauce: In a small bowl, whisk together the Greek yogurt, lemon juice, tahini, minced garlic, chopped parsley, salt, and pepper until smooth and well combined. Adjust seasoning to taste. Cover and refrigerate until ready to serve.
3. Cook the Chicken: Heat a large skillet over medium-high heat. Add the marinated chicken thighs to the skillet and cook for 6-8 minutes, stirring occasionally, until the chicken is cooked through and nicely browned. Remove from heat and set aside.
4. Warm the Pita Bread: Heat the pita bread rounds in a toaster oven or microwave until warm and soft.
5. Assemble the Pitas: Spread a generous spoonful of yogurt sauce onto each warm pita bread round. Top with a portion of the cooked chicken shawarma. Add sliced tomatoes, sliced cucumbers, thinly sliced red onion, chopped parsley or cilantro, and pickles (if using).
6. Serve: Fold the Chicken Shawarma Pitas in half and serve immediately.

Enjoy these delicious Chicken Shawarma Pitas as a satisfying and flavorful meal for lunch or dinner! Adjust the toppings and seasonings to suit your taste preferences.

Thai Basil Chicken Rice Bowl

Ingredients:

For the Thai Basil Chicken:

- 1 lb boneless, skinless chicken breasts or thighs, thinly sliced
- 2 tablespoons vegetable oil
- 4 cloves garlic, minced
- 2 Thai bird's eye chilies, thinly sliced (adjust to taste)
- 1 bell pepper, thinly sliced
- 1 onion, thinly sliced
- 1 cup fresh Thai basil leaves
- 2 tablespoons oyster sauce
- 1 tablespoon soy sauce
- 1 tablespoon fish sauce
- 1 tablespoon sugar
- Juice of 1 lime

For the Rice Bowl:

- Cooked jasmine rice or brown rice
- Sliced cucumber
- Sliced cherry tomatoes
- Sliced avocado
- Thinly sliced red onion
- Lime wedges, for serving
- Fresh cilantro, for garnish
- Crushed peanuts, for garnish (optional)

Instructions:

1. Prepare the Thai Basil Chicken: Heat the vegetable oil in a large skillet or wok over medium-high heat. Add the minced garlic and sliced Thai bird's eye chilies, and stir-fry for about 30 seconds until fragrant.
2. Add the thinly sliced chicken to the skillet and cook, stirring frequently, until the chicken is cooked through and no longer pink.
3. Stir in the sliced bell pepper and onion, and continue to cook for another 2-3 minutes until the vegetables are tender-crisp.
4. Add the oyster sauce, soy sauce, fish sauce, and sugar to the skillet. Stir well to combine and coat the chicken and vegetables evenly with the sauce.

5. Remove the skillet from heat and stir in the fresh Thai basil leaves and lime juice. Toss everything together until the basil wilts slightly.
6. Assemble the Rice Bowl: Divide the cooked jasmine rice or brown rice among serving bowls. Top each bowl with a portion of the Thai basil chicken mixture.
7. Arrange sliced cucumber, sliced cherry tomatoes, sliced avocado, and thinly sliced red onion around the chicken.
8. Garnish and Serve: Garnish the Thai Basil Chicken Rice Bowls with fresh cilantro and crushed peanuts (if using). Serve with lime wedges on the side for squeezing over the rice bowl.
9. Enjoy your flavorful and aromatic Thai Basil Chicken Rice Bowl!

Feel free to customize your Thai Basil Chicken Rice Bowl with additional toppings such as sliced bell peppers, shredded carrots, or chopped scallions. Adjust the level of spiciness by adding more or fewer Thai bird's eye chilies according to your preference.

Mexican Churros with Chocolate Sauce

Ingredients:

For the Churros:

- 1 cup water
- 1/2 cup unsalted butter
- 2 tablespoons granulated sugar
- 1/4 teaspoon salt
- 1 cup all-purpose flour
- 2 large eggs
- 1 teaspoon vanilla extract
- Vegetable oil, for frying

For the Cinnamon Sugar Coating:

- 1/2 cup granulated sugar
- 1 teaspoon ground cinnamon

For the Chocolate Sauce:

- 4 ounces semi-sweet chocolate, chopped
- 1/2 cup heavy cream
- 1 tablespoon unsalted butter
- 1/2 teaspoon vanilla extract
- Pinch of salt

Instructions:

1. Make the Churro Dough: In a saucepan, combine water, butter, sugar, and salt. Bring to a boil over medium heat, stirring occasionally. Remove from heat and add the flour all at once. Stir vigorously until the mixture forms a smooth dough.
2. Transfer the dough to a mixing bowl and let it cool for a few minutes. Add the eggs, one at a time, mixing well after each addition. Stir in the vanilla extract until well combined.
3. Fry the Churros: Heat vegetable oil in a deep fryer or large pot to 375°F (190°C). Spoon the churro dough into a piping bag fitted with a large star tip.
4. Pipe 4-5 inch strips of dough directly into the hot oil, using scissors or a knife to cut the dough. Fry the churros for 2-3 minutes on each side, or until golden brown and crispy. Remove from the oil and drain on paper towels.

5. Coat the Churros: In a shallow bowl, mix together the granulated sugar and ground cinnamon. Roll the fried churros in the cinnamon sugar mixture until well coated.
6. Make the Chocolate Sauce: In a small saucepan, heat the heavy cream until it just begins to simmer. Remove from heat and add the chopped chocolate, butter, vanilla extract, and a pinch of salt. Stir until the chocolate is melted and the sauce is smooth.
7. Serve: Serve the warm churros with the chocolate sauce for dipping.
8. Enjoy your delicious Mexican Churros with Chocolate Sauce!

These churros are best enjoyed fresh and warm. You can also customize them by dusting them with powdered sugar or serving them with caramel sauce instead of chocolate.

Cuban Tostones with Garlic Sauce

Ingredients:

For the Tostones:

- 2 green plantains, peeled and cut into 1-inch thick slices
- Vegetable oil, for frying
- Salt, to taste

For the Garlic Sauce:

- 4 cloves garlic, minced
- 1/4 cup extra virgin olive oil
- 2 tablespoons fresh lime juice
- Salt and pepper, to taste
- Chopped fresh cilantro or parsley, for garnish

Instructions:

1. Prepare the Tostones: Heat vegetable oil in a large skillet or deep fryer over medium-high heat. Fry the plantain slices in batches for 2-3 minutes on each side, or until golden brown and tender.
2. Remove the fried plantains from the oil and drain on paper towels. Using a tostonera (plantain press) or the bottom of a flat glass, flatten each fried plantain slice to about 1/4 inch thickness.
3. Return the flattened plantains to the hot oil and fry for an additional 2-3 minutes on each side, or until crispy and golden brown. Remove from the oil and drain on paper towels. Season with salt to taste.
4. Make the Garlic Sauce: In a small saucepan, heat the extra virgin olive oil over medium heat. Add the minced garlic and cook for 1-2 minutes, stirring constantly, until fragrant. Be careful not to burn the garlic.
5. Remove the saucepan from heat and stir in the fresh lime juice. Season with salt and pepper to taste.
6. Serve: Arrange the crispy tostones on a serving platter and drizzle with the garlic sauce. Garnish with chopped fresh cilantro or parsley.
7. Enjoy your flavorful Cuban Tostones with Garlic Sauce as a delicious appetizer or side dish!

These tostones are best served hot and crispy, straight from the fryer. The garlic sauce adds a delicious burst of flavor, making them irresistible. Feel free to adjust the amount of garlic and lime juice in the sauce according to your taste preferences.

Greek Souvlaki Skewers

Ingredients:

For the Marinade:

- 1/4 cup extra virgin olive oil
- 1/4 cup fresh lemon juice
- 2 cloves garlic, minced
- 1 teaspoon dried oregano
- 1 teaspoon dried thyme
- 1 teaspoon dried rosemary
- Salt and pepper, to taste

For the Skewers:

- 1 lb boneless, skinless chicken breasts or thighs, cut into 1-inch cubes
- 1 red bell pepper, cut into chunks
- 1 yellow bell pepper, cut into chunks
- 1 red onion, cut into chunks
- Cherry tomatoes
- Wooden skewers, soaked in water for at least 30 minutes

For Serving:

- Greek yogurt tzatziki sauce
- Pita bread
- Sliced cucumbers
- Sliced tomatoes
- Sliced red onion
- Chopped fresh parsley or dill
- Lemon wedges

Instructions:

1. Prepare the Marinade: In a small bowl, whisk together the extra virgin olive oil, fresh lemon juice, minced garlic, dried oregano, dried thyme, dried rosemary, salt, and pepper.
2. Marinate the Chicken: Place the chicken cubes in a large resealable plastic bag or shallow dish. Pour the marinade over the chicken and toss to coat evenly. Seal

the bag or cover the dish and marinate in the refrigerator for at least 30 minutes, or up to 4 hours.
3. Assemble the Skewers: Preheat the grill or grill pan over medium-high heat. Thread the marinated chicken cubes, bell pepper chunks, red onion chunks, and cherry tomatoes onto the soaked wooden skewers, alternating the ingredients as desired.
4. Grill the Skewers: Place the assembled skewers on the preheated grill or grill pan. Grill for 8-10 minutes, turning occasionally, until the chicken is cooked through and the vegetables are tender and slightly charred.
5. Serve: Remove the cooked skewers from the grill and transfer them to a serving platter. Serve the Greek Souvlaki Skewers with Greek yogurt tzatziki sauce, pita bread, sliced cucumbers, sliced tomatoes, sliced red onion, chopped fresh parsley or dill, and lemon wedges on the side.
6. Enjoy your delicious Greek Souvlaki Skewers as a flavorful and satisfying meal!

These Greek Souvlaki Skewers are perfect for summer grilling or as a crowd-pleasing dish for gatherings and parties. Feel free to customize the skewers with your favorite vegetables and serve them with your choice of sides and toppings.

Korean Bibimbap Bowls

Ingredients:

For the Bibimbap:

- 2 cups cooked short-grain rice
- 1 cup spinach
- 1 cup bean sprouts
- 1 medium carrot, julienned
- 1/2 cup sliced shiitake mushrooms
- 1/2 cup sliced cucumber
- 2 cups cooked protein of choice (sliced beef, chicken, or tofu)
- 4 eggs
- Sesame oil, for frying
- Salt, to taste
- Sesame seeds, for garnish

For the Bibimbap Sauce (Gochujang Sauce):

- 4 tablespoons gochujang (Korean chili paste)
- 2 tablespoons sesame oil
- 2 tablespoons soy sauce
- 2 tablespoons rice vinegar
- 1 tablespoon honey or sugar
- 1 clove garlic, minced
- 1 teaspoon grated ginger
- 2 tablespoons water (adjust for desired consistency)

Instructions:

1. Prepare the Bibimbap Sauce: In a small bowl, whisk together the gochujang, sesame oil, soy sauce, rice vinegar, honey or sugar, minced garlic, grated ginger, and water until smooth. Adjust the amount of water for desired consistency. Set aside.
2. Cook the Vegetables: Blanch the spinach and bean sprouts in boiling water for 1-2 minutes, then drain and rinse under cold water. Squeeze out excess water from the blanched spinach and bean sprouts, then season each with a pinch of salt and a drizzle of sesame oil. Sauté the julienned carrot and sliced shiitake mushrooms in a pan with a little sesame oil until tender. Set aside.

3. Cook the Protein: Season the protein of choice (sliced beef, chicken, or tofu) with salt and any desired seasonings. Cook in a pan with a little sesame oil until browned and cooked through. Set aside.
4. Fry the Eggs: Heat a little sesame oil in a non-stick skillet over medium heat. Crack the eggs into the skillet and cook until the whites are set but the yolks are still runny. Remove from heat and set aside.
5. Assemble the Bibimbap Bowls: Divide the cooked rice among serving bowls. Arrange the blanched spinach, bean sprouts, sautéed carrot and shiitake mushrooms, sliced cucumber, and cooked protein on top of the rice in separate sections.
6. Top each bowl with a fried egg.
7. Garnish with sesame seeds.
8. Serve with the Bibimbap sauce on the side.
9. Mix everything together just before eating, adding the Bibimbap sauce according to your taste preference.

Enjoy your flavorful and nutritious Korean Bibimbap Bowls! Adjust the toppings and protein according to your preferences.

BBQ Rib Sliders

Ingredients:

For the BBQ Ribs:

- 1 rack of baby back ribs
- Salt and pepper, to taste
- BBQ sauce of your choice

For the Sliders:

- Slider buns or dinner rolls
- Coleslaw (store-bought or homemade)
- Pickles, optional

Instructions:

1. Prepare the Ribs: Preheat your grill to medium-high heat. Season the rack of baby back ribs generously with salt and pepper.
2. Place the ribs on the grill and cook for about 3-4 minutes per side, until nicely browned and grill marks appear.
3. Reduce the heat to medium-low, close the lid, and continue cooking the ribs for about 1-1.5 hours, or until tender. You can also use a smoker or oven for cooking the ribs at a low temperature (around 275°F or 135°C) for 3-4 hours until tender.
4. Baste the ribs with BBQ sauce during the last 15-20 minutes of cooking, brushing it on both sides and allowing it to caramelize.
5. Once the ribs are cooked and tender, remove them from the grill or smoker and let them rest for a few minutes before slicing into individual ribs.
6. Assemble the Sliders: Slice the slider buns or dinner rolls in half. Place a generous amount of coleslaw on the bottom half of each bun. Top with a rib or two, depending on the size of your buns. Add a pickle slice if desired.
7. Place the top half of the bun over the rib and secure with a toothpick if necessary.
8. Serve: Arrange the BBQ Rib Sliders on a platter and serve immediately. Enjoy!

These BBQ Rib Sliders are perfect for parties, game day, or any casual gathering. They're easy to make and packed with flavor, making them a crowd-pleasing appetizer or main course. Feel free to customize the sliders with your favorite BBQ sauce or additional toppings like onions or jalapeños.

Vegetarian Spring Rolls with Peanut Sauce

Ingredients:

For the Spring Rolls:

- 8-10 rice paper wrappers
- 2 cups cooked vermicelli rice noodles
- 1 cup shredded carrots
- 1 cup thinly sliced cucumber
- 1 cup thinly sliced bell peppers (red, yellow, or orange)
- 1 cup shredded purple cabbage
- 1 cup fresh cilantro leaves
- 1 cup fresh mint leaves
- 1 cup fresh basil leaves
- 1 cup bean sprouts (optional)
- Lime wedges, for serving (optional)

For the Peanut Sauce:

- 1/4 cup creamy peanut butter
- 2 tablespoons soy sauce
- 2 tablespoons rice vinegar
- 1 tablespoon honey or maple syrup
- 1 clove garlic, minced
- 1 teaspoon grated ginger
- 1-2 tablespoons warm water, as needed to thin the sauce
- Crushed peanuts, for garnish (optional)

Instructions:

1. Prepare the Peanut Sauce: In a small bowl, whisk together the peanut butter, soy sauce, rice vinegar, honey or maple syrup, minced garlic, and grated ginger until smooth. Add warm water, 1 tablespoon at a time, until the sauce reaches your desired consistency. Set aside.
2. Prepare the Rice Paper Wrappers: Fill a shallow dish or large bowl with warm water. Dip one rice paper wrapper into the water for about 10-15 seconds until it softens and becomes pliable. Remove from the water and place it flat on a clean work surface.
3. Assemble the Spring Rolls: Place a small handful of cooked vermicelli rice noodles in the center of the softened rice paper wrapper. Top with shredded

carrots, sliced cucumber, sliced bell peppers, shredded purple cabbage, fresh cilantro leaves, fresh mint leaves, fresh basil leaves, and bean sprouts (if using).
4. Roll the Spring Rolls: Fold the bottom edge of the rice paper wrapper over the filling, then fold in the sides, and roll tightly to enclose the filling completely. Repeat with the remaining ingredients to make more spring rolls.
5. Serve the Spring Rolls: Arrange the Vegetarian Spring Rolls on a serving platter. Garnish with crushed peanuts if desired. Serve with the prepared Peanut Sauce for dipping and lime wedges on the side.
6. Enjoy your delicious Vegetarian Spring Rolls with Peanut Sauce as a refreshing appetizer or light meal!

Feel free to customize the spring rolls with your favorite vegetables, herbs, or protein options like tofu or tempeh. You can also add avocado slices or mango strips for extra flavor and texture. Adjust the sweetness and spiciness of the peanut sauce according to your taste preference.

Cajun Gumbo

Ingredients:

For the Roux:

- 1/2 cup all-purpose flour
- 1/2 cup vegetable oil

For the Gumbo:

- 1 lb andouille sausage, sliced
- 1 lb chicken thighs, boneless and skinless, diced
- 1 large onion, diced
- 1 bell pepper, diced
- 2 celery stalks, diced
- 4 cloves garlic, minced
- 4 cups chicken broth
- 1 (14.5 oz) can diced tomatoes
- 1 cup okra, sliced (fresh or frozen)
- 2 bay leaves
- 1 teaspoon dried thyme
- 1 teaspoon dried oregano
- 1 teaspoon paprika
- 1/2 teaspoon cayenne pepper (adjust to taste)
- Salt and black pepper, to taste
- Cooked white rice, for serving
- Chopped green onions, for garnish

Instructions:

1. Make the Roux: In a large, heavy-bottomed pot or Dutch oven, heat the vegetable oil over medium heat. Gradually whisk in the flour to form a smooth paste. Cook the roux, stirring constantly, for about 20-30 minutes or until it turns a dark brown color. Be careful not to burn the roux.
2. Cook the Sausage and Chicken: Once the roux reaches the desired color, add the sliced andouille sausage to the pot. Cook, stirring occasionally, until the sausage is browned. Remove the sausage from the pot and set aside. In the same pot, add the diced chicken thighs and cook until browned on all sides. Remove the chicken from the pot and set aside.

3. Sauté the Vegetables: Add the diced onion, bell pepper, celery, and minced garlic to the pot. Sauté the vegetables until they are softened and fragrant, about 5-7 minutes.
4. Simmer the Gumbo: Return the cooked sausage and chicken to the pot. Pour in the chicken broth and diced tomatoes with their juices. Stir in the sliced okra, bay leaves, dried thyme, dried oregano, paprika, and cayenne pepper. Season with salt and black pepper to taste.
5. Bring the mixture to a simmer, then reduce the heat to low. Cover and let the gumbo simmer for about 1 hour, stirring occasionally, until the flavors meld together and the gumbo thickens slightly.
6. Serve: Remove the bay leaves from the gumbo. Ladle the Cajun Gumbo over cooked white rice in serving bowls. Garnish with chopped green onions before serving.
7. Enjoy your flavorful Cajun Gumbo with rice and crusty bread on the side!

Feel free to customize this Cajun Gumbo recipe by adding other ingredients like shrimp, crab, or chopped okra. Adjust the spices to suit your taste preferences for a spicier or milder gumbo.

Beef Barbacoa Tacos

Ingredients:

For the Beef Barbacoa:

- 2 lbs beef chuck roast or beef brisket, cut into large chunks
- 4 cloves garlic, minced
- 1 onion, finely chopped
- 2 chipotle peppers in adobo sauce, chopped
- 1 tablespoon adobo sauce (from the canned chipotle peppers)
- 1/4 cup lime juice
- 1/4 cup apple cider vinegar
- 1/4 cup beef broth or water
- 2 teaspoons ground cumin
- 2 teaspoons dried oregano
- 2 teaspoons smoked paprika
- 1 teaspoon ground coriander
- 1 teaspoon salt
- 1/2 teaspoon black pepper

For Serving:

- Corn or flour tortillas
- Chopped fresh cilantro
- Diced onion
- Sliced radishes
- Lime wedges
- Salsa or hot sauce (optional)

Instructions:

1. Prepare the Beef Barbacoa: In a bowl, mix together the minced garlic, chopped onion, chopped chipotle peppers, adobo sauce, lime juice, apple cider vinegar, beef broth or water, ground cumin, dried oregano, smoked paprika, ground coriander, salt, and black pepper.
2. Place the beef chunks in a slow cooker or Instant Pot. Pour the marinade over the beef and toss to coat evenly.
3. Cook the Beef:
    - For a Slow Cooker: Cover and cook on low heat for 6-8 hours or high heat for 3-4 hours, or until the beef is tender and easily shreds with a fork.

- For an Instant Pot: Seal the Instant Pot and cook on high pressure for 60 minutes. Let the pressure release naturally for 10 minutes, then manually release any remaining pressure.
4. Once the beef is cooked, use two forks to shred it into smaller pieces. Toss the shredded beef in the cooking juices to coat.
5. Assemble the Tacos: Heat the tortillas in a dry skillet or microwave until warm and pliable. Spoon the shredded beef onto each tortilla. Top with chopped cilantro, diced onion, sliced radishes, and a squeeze of lime juice.
6. Serve the Beef Barbacoa Tacos immediately with salsa or hot sauce on the side, if desired.
7. Enjoy your flavorful Beef Barbacoa Tacos!

Feel free to customize your tacos with additional toppings such as avocado slices, shredded lettuce, diced tomatoes, or crumbled cheese. Adjust the spice level of the chipotle peppers and adobo sauce to suit your taste preferences.

Vietnamese Pho Soup

Ingredients:

For the Broth:

- 2 large onions, halved
- 4-inch piece of ginger, halved lengthwise
- 4-5 lbs beef bones (such as oxtail, marrow bones, or knuckle bones)
- 2 cinnamon sticks
- 4 star anise
- 6 whole cloves
- 1 black cardamom pod (optional)
- 1 tablespoon coriander seeds
- 1 tablespoon fennel seeds
- 1 tablespoon salt
- 1 tablespoon sugar
- Water

For Serving:

- 1 lb rice noodles (banh pho)
- Thinly sliced raw beef (such as sirloin or eye of round)
- Bean sprouts
- Fresh Thai basil leaves
- Fresh cilantro leaves
- Thinly sliced green onions
- Lime wedges
- Sliced jalapenos
- Hoisin sauce
- Sriracha or chili sauce

Instructions:

1. Prepare the Broth: Preheat the oven to 425°F (220°C). Place the halved onions and ginger on a baking sheet and roast in the oven for about 20-30 minutes, or until charred and aromatic.
2. In a large stockpot, add the beef bones and enough water to cover them. Bring to a boil over high heat and let it boil vigorously for about 10 minutes to remove any impurities. Drain the bones and rinse them under cold water.

3. Place the cleaned bones back in the pot and add the roasted onions and ginger, along with the cinnamon sticks, star anise, cloves, black cardamom pod (if using), coriander seeds, fennel seeds, salt, and sugar.
4. Fill the pot with enough water to cover the bones and spices, about 4-5 quarts. Bring to a boil over high heat, then reduce the heat to low and let the broth simmer gently, uncovered, for at least 4 hours, preferably 6-8 hours, skimming off any foam and impurities that rise to the surface.
5. Strain the broth through a fine-mesh sieve or cheesecloth into a clean pot or large bowl. Discard the solids. Taste the broth and adjust the seasoning with more salt or sugar if needed.
6. Prepare the Noodles and Beef: Cook the rice noodles according to the package instructions. Thinly slice the raw beef against the grain. The beef will cook in the hot broth.
7. Assemble the Pho Soup: Divide the cooked noodles among serving bowls. Top with thinly sliced raw beef. Ladle the hot broth over the noodles and beef, ensuring that the beef is submerged in the hot broth to cook.
8. Serve the pho with a plate of bean sprouts, Thai basil leaves, cilantro leaves, sliced green onions, lime wedges, sliced jalapenos, hoisin sauce, and sriracha or chili sauce on the side for diners to customize their bowls according to their taste preferences.
9. Enjoy your delicious Vietnamese Pho Soup!

Pho is a versatile dish, so feel free to customize it with your favorite protein options like cooked beef brisket, meatballs, or chicken. Adjust the garnishes and condiments according to your taste preferences.

Loaded Tater Tots

Ingredients:

- 1 (32 oz) bag frozen tater tots
- 1 cup shredded cheddar cheese
- 1/2 cup cooked and crumbled bacon
- 1/4 cup chopped green onions
- Sour cream, for serving
- Ketchup or your favorite dipping sauce, for serving

Instructions:

1. Bake the Tater Tots: Preheat your oven according to the instructions on the tater tots package. Arrange the frozen tater tots in a single layer on a baking sheet lined with parchment paper or aluminum foil.
2. Bake the tater tots according to the package instructions until they are golden brown and crispy.
3. Assemble the Loaded Tater Tots: Remove the baked tater tots from the oven and transfer them to a serving platter or individual plates. Sprinkle the shredded cheddar cheese evenly over the hot tater tots, allowing the cheese to melt slightly.
4. Scatter the cooked and crumbled bacon pieces over the melted cheese. Sprinkle chopped green onions over the top of the loaded tater tots.
5. Serve: Serve the loaded tater tots immediately while they are hot and cheesy. Offer sour cream and ketchup or your favorite dipping sauce on the side for dipping.
6. Enjoy your delicious Loaded Tater Tots as a fun and satisfying appetizer or snack!

Feel free to customize your loaded tater tots with additional toppings such as diced tomatoes, sliced jalapenos, sliced black olives, or diced avocado. You can also experiment with different types of cheese or add cooked ground beef or shredded chicken for extra protein.

Jerk Chicken Wraps

Ingredients:

For the Jerk Chicken:

- 1 lb boneless, skinless chicken breasts or thighs
- 3 tablespoons jerk seasoning (store-bought or homemade)
- 2 tablespoons olive oil

For the Wraps:

- Large flour tortillas or wraps
- Shredded lettuce
- Sliced tomatoes
- Sliced red onions
- Sliced avocado
- Fresh cilantro leaves
- Lime wedges, for serving (optional)

For the Jerk Sauce:

- 1/4 cup mayonnaise
- 2 tablespoons plain Greek yogurt or sour cream
- 1 tablespoon jerk seasoning
- 1 tablespoon lime juice
- 1 teaspoon honey
- Salt and pepper, to taste

Instructions:

1. Marinate the Chicken: In a bowl, combine the chicken with the jerk seasoning and olive oil. Mix well to coat the chicken evenly. Cover and refrigerate for at least 30 minutes, or up to 4 hours, to allow the flavors to marinate.
2. Cook the Chicken: Heat a grill pan or skillet over medium-high heat. Cook the marinated chicken for 5-6 minutes per side, or until cooked through and nicely charred on the outside. Remove from heat and let it rest for a few minutes before slicing.
3. Prepare the Jerk Sauce: In a small bowl, whisk together the mayonnaise, Greek yogurt or sour cream, jerk seasoning, lime juice, honey, salt, and pepper until smooth. Adjust the seasoning to taste.

4. Assemble the Wraps: Lay a flour tortilla or wrap flat on a clean work surface. Spread a generous amount of the jerk sauce over the tortilla. Top with shredded lettuce, sliced tomatoes, sliced red onions, sliced avocado, fresh cilantro leaves, and sliced jerk chicken.
5. Fold the sides of the tortilla inwards, then roll it up tightly to form a wrap. Secure the wrap with toothpicks if needed.
6. Serve the Jerk Chicken Wraps immediately with lime wedges on the side for squeezing over the wraps, if desired.
7. Enjoy your flavorful Jerk Chicken Wraps as a delicious and satisfying meal!

Feel free to customize your Jerk Chicken Wraps with additional toppings such as sliced bell peppers, shredded cheese, or diced mango for a tropical twist. Adjust the level of spiciness in the jerk seasoning and sauce according to your taste preferences.

Caprese Panini

Ingredients:

- 4 ciabatta rolls or sandwich bread slices
- 2 large ripe tomatoes, sliced
- 8 oz fresh mozzarella cheese, sliced
- 1/2 cup fresh basil leaves
- Balsamic glaze or balsamic reduction (store-bought or homemade)
- Olive oil, for brushing
- Salt and pepper, to taste

Instructions:

1. Preheat the Panini Press: Preheat your Panini press according to the manufacturer's instructions.
2. Prepare the Ingredients: Slice the ciabatta rolls horizontally to create top and bottom halves. If using sandwich bread slices, you can leave them as is. Slice the tomatoes and fresh mozzarella cheese into thin slices. Wash and dry the fresh basil leaves.
3. Assemble the Panini: On the bottom half of each ciabatta roll or sandwich bread slice, layer slices of tomato, fresh mozzarella cheese, and fresh basil leaves. Season with salt and pepper to taste. Drizzle a little balsamic glaze or balsamic reduction over the ingredients.
4. Top with the Remaining Bread: Place the top half of each ciabatta roll or another slice of sandwich bread over the filling to create sandwiches.
5. Grill the Panini: Brush the outsides of the sandwiches lightly with olive oil. Place the sandwiches on the preheated Panini press and close the lid. Grill for 4-5 minutes, or until the bread is golden brown and crispy, and the cheese is melted.
6. Serve: Remove the Caprese Panini from the Panini press and let them cool for a minute or two. Slice each Panini in half diagonally and serve warm.
7. Enjoy your delicious Caprese Panini with a side salad or your favorite soup for a satisfying meal!

Feel free to customize your Caprese Panini by adding ingredients like roasted red peppers, avocado slices, or prosciutto for extra flavor and texture. Adjust the amount of balsamic glaze or reduction according to your taste preferences.

Hawaiian Spam Musubi

Ingredients:

- 1 can Spam
- 2 cups sushi rice (prepared according to package instructions)
- 1/4 cup soy sauce
- 1/4 cup sugar
- 2 tablespoons rice vinegar
- 4-5 sheets nori (seaweed), cut in half
- Furikake (optional, for sprinkling on the rice)
- Plastic wrap or wax paper
- Musubi mold (optional, can use the Spam can as a mold)

Instructions:

1. Cook the Rice: Prepare the sushi rice according to the package instructions. Once cooked, mix in the rice vinegar. Keep the rice covered and warm.
2. Prepare the Spam: Remove the Spam from the can and slice it into 8-10 equal pieces.
3. Make the Sauce: In a small bowl, mix the soy sauce and sugar together until the sugar is dissolved.
4. Cook the Spam: Heat a non-stick skillet over medium heat. Add the Spam slices and cook until lightly browned on both sides. Pour the soy sauce mixture over the Spam slices and cook until the sauce has thickened and the Spam is well-coated. Remove from heat.
5. Assemble the Musubi:
    - Using a Musubi Mold: Place a piece of nori on a clean surface. Place the musubi mold in the center of the nori. Fill the mold with about 1/4 cup of sushi rice, pressing it down firmly. Sprinkle with furikake if using. Place a slice of Spam on top of the rice. Add another thin layer of rice on top of the Spam, pressing down firmly again. Remove the mold.
    - Without a Musubi Mold: Line the inside of the Spam can with plastic wrap, leaving enough overhang to lift the rice out later. Layer the rice and Spam in the can as described above, pressing down firmly with each layer. Lift the musubi out using the plastic wrap.
6. Wrap the Nori: Fold the nori over the top of the rice and Spam stack, using a bit of water to seal the edges of the nori.
7. Serve: Let the musubi sit for a minute to allow the nori to soften slightly. Cut each musubi in half, if desired, and serve.

8. Enjoy your Hawaiian Spam Musubi as a delicious snack or meal!

Feel free to customize your Spam Musubi by adding a layer of scrambled eggs, avocado slices, or pickled vegetables. Adjust the sweetness and saltiness of the soy sauce mixture to suit your taste preferences.

Thai Mango Sticky Rice

Ingredients:

For the Sticky Rice:

- 1 cup glutinous rice (also known as sticky rice or sweet rice)
- 1 1/4 cups coconut milk
- 1/4 cup sugar
- 1/4 teaspoon salt

For the Sauce:

- 1/2 cup coconut milk
- 1 tablespoon sugar
- 1/4 teaspoon salt
- 1 teaspoon cornstarch mixed with 1 tablespoon water (optional, for thickening)

For Serving:

- 2 ripe mangoes, peeled and sliced
- Toasted sesame seeds or mung beans (optional, for garnish)

Instructions:

1. Prepare the Sticky Rice:
    - Rinse the glutinous rice under cold water until the water runs clear. Soak the rice in water for at least 4 hours or overnight.
    - Drain the soaked rice and steam it in a bamboo steamer or a heatproof dish set over boiling water. Steam for about 20-25 minutes, or until the rice is tender and sticky.
2. Make the Coconut Milk Mixture:
    - While the rice is steaming, combine 1 1/4 cups of coconut milk, 1/4 cup of sugar, and 1/4 teaspoon of salt in a saucepan. Cook over low heat, stirring frequently, until the sugar is dissolved and the mixture is warm (do not boil).
3. Combine the Rice and Coconut Milk:
    - Once the rice is cooked, transfer it to a large bowl. Pour the warm coconut milk mixture over the rice and stir to combine. Cover and let it sit for about 20-30 minutes, or until the rice has absorbed the coconut milk.
4. Make the Sauce:

- In a small saucepan, combine 1/2 cup of coconut milk, 1 tablespoon of sugar, and 1/4 teaspoon of salt. Cook over low heat, stirring frequently, until the sugar is dissolved and the mixture is warm. If you prefer a thicker sauce, add the cornstarch mixture and cook until the sauce thickens slightly.
5. Prepare the Mangoes:
    - Peel the mangoes and slice them into thin pieces or cubes.
6. Serve:
    - To serve, place a portion of the sticky rice on a serving plate. Arrange the mango slices next to the rice. Drizzle some of the coconut sauce over the sticky rice. Garnish with toasted sesame seeds or mung beans, if desired.
7. Enjoy your Thai Mango Sticky Rice!

Feel free to adjust the sweetness and saltiness of the coconut milk mixture and sauce to suit your taste preferences. This delightful dessert is best enjoyed fresh, but it can also be served at room temperature.

www.ingramcontent.com/pod-product-compliance
Lightning Source LLC
LaVergne TN
LVHW081607060526
838201LV00054B/2126